teach yourself

triathlon
steve trew

Launched in 1938, the **teach yourself** series
grew rapidly in response to the world's wartime
needs. Loved and trusted by over 50 million
readers, the series has continued to respond to
society's changing interests and passions and
now, 70 years on, includes over 500 titles,
from Arabic and Beekeeping to Yoga and Zulu.
What would you like to learn?

be where you want to be with **teach yourself**

For UK order enquiries: please contact Bookpoint Ltd, 130 Milton Park, Abingdon, Oxon OX14 4SB. Telephone: +44 (0) 1235 827720. Fax: +44 (0) 1235 400454. Lines are open 09.00–17.00, Monday to Saturday, with a 24-hour message answering service. Details about our titles and how to order are available at www.teachyourself.co.uk

For USA order enquiries: please contact McGraw-Hill Customer Services, PO Box 545, Blacklick, OH 43004-0545, USA. Telephone: 1-800-722-4726. Fax: 1-614-755-5645.

For Canada order enquiries: please contact McGraw-Hill Ryerson Ltd, 300 Water St, Whitby, Ontario L1N 9B6, Canada. Telephone: 905 430 5000. Fax: 905 430 5020.

Long renowned as the authoritative source for self-guided learning – with more than 50 million copies sold worldwide – the **teach yourself** series includes over 500 titles in the fields of languages, crafts, hobbies, business, computing and education.

British Library Cataloguing in Publication Data: a catalogue record for this title is available from the British Library.

Library of Congress Catalog Card Number: on file.

First published in UK 2008 by Hodder Education, part of Hachette UK, 338 Euston Road, London NW1 3BH.

First published in US 2008 by The McGraw-Hill Companies, Inc.

This edition published 2008.

The **teach yourself** name is a registered trade mark of Hodder Headline.

Copyright © 2008 Steve Trew
Consultant Editor: Sara Kirkham

Typeset by Transet Limited, Coventry, England.
Printed in Great Britain for Hodder Education, an Hachette UK Company, 338 Euston Road, London NW1 3BH, by CPI Cox & Wyman, Reading, Berkshire RG1 8EX.

The publisher has used its best endeavours to ensure that the URLs for external websites referred to in this book are correct and active at the time of going to press. However, the publisher and the author have no responsibility for the websites and can make no guarantee that a site will remain live or that the content will remain relevant, decent or appropriate.

Hachette UK's policy is to use papers that are natural, renewable and recyclable products and made from wood grown in sustainable forests. The logging and manufacturing processes are expected to conform to the environmental regulations of the country of origin.

Impression number   10 9 8 7 6 5 4 3 2 1
Year   2012 2011 2010 2009 2008

iii

contents

about the author

Steve Trew is one of the best-known names in triathlon as a coach, race commentator, journalist and novelist. He has coached medallists at European and World Championships and was at the Sydney Olympic Games as part of the British coaching team and also as race commentator for triathlon.

In 2002, he was the race commentator at the Commonwealth Games for both triathlon and swimming. In 2004, he was BBC TV commentator for the Athens Olympic Games. In 2006, Steve was team manager for the Commonwealth Games for Wales Triathlon. He has also provided live commentary at the London Marathon to add to his list of credits. He was previously Director of Coaching and National Coach for Great Britain.

He has extensive experience of working with squads of International, non-International, senior and junior squads, and mixed squads, and has a special interest in social and group dynamics and diametrics and its application to working with squads.

Steve has organized triathlon training camps since 1984 in Great Britain and since 1987 in many parts of the world including Mexico; Madras, India; Karatas, Yugoslavia; Israel; South Africa: Durban, Stellenbosch and Pretoria; Saudi Arabia; Northern and Southern Ireland; Hong Kong; Malta; Bermuda and Australia.

He has coached extensively abroad for National Federations, and the IOC and ITU on Olympic solidarity camps.

Having set up, organized and written the original syllabus for the BTA coach education scheme and taken responsibility for instigating the courses, Steve has also developed coach education in Ireland, Hong Kong, Yugoslavia, Israel and South Africa.

As well as the Olympic and Commonwealth Games, Steve has commentated at many ITU World Cup events and World Championships in Wellington, New Zealand; Cancun, Mexico; Perth, Australia (twice); and Edmonton, Canada. He was also commentator at the World Duathlon championships in Cancun, Mexico; Ferrarra, Italy; Gernika, Spain; and the long-course Duathlon Worlds in Venray, Holland.

Books/Publications:

Triathlon: skills of the game (Crowood Press)

Triathlon: a training manual (Crowood press)

Triathlon: a long day's dying (W publishing)

Triathlon: a moment of suffering (Wednesday press)

Skills of Triathlon DVD (Crowood press)

Steve can be contached at trew@personalbest.demon.co.uk

Steve works closely with Dan Bullock from SwimforTri and would wish to thank him for his massive input into the swimming sections.

introduction

Triathlon is the sport of the twenty-first century. It is a sport that combines the three individual disciplines of swimming, cycling and running immediately after each other without a break. The changeover between the three disciplines is a part of the sport in its own right and is called the transition. It is often referred to as 'the fourth discipline'.

After the running and marathon boom in the late seventies and eighties had attracted many new people into sport and a healthier lifestyle, triathlon became the next natural step for those looking for a new challenge. Over the last 20 years, triathlon has become a popular sport to be involved with, and reports have indicated that it could be the fastest-growing sport in the UK.

There still remains that feeling of being a little outside of the 'normal' sports, a feeling that you are exploring new areas and new limits of training, but triathlon is a friendly sport. Experienced triathletes will be willing to help and advise you. There are many triathlon clubs all over the country and they welcome new members. When you are ready, join a club; it will make training more sociable, more fun and probably more directed.

This book is a great starting point if you have just enrolled for your first triathlon or are considering taking it up. It will also be useful if you have already completed a few triathlons but want to improve your performance, or discover some useful insider tips to knock a few all-important seconds off your race time.

Throughout this book you will find training programmes for each of the three disciplines and tips on that crucial transition, as well as:

- information on what kit you need (and what you don't need)
- essential information on the open water swim
- how to train for more than one discipline with back-to-back and brick training
- advice on diet and supplementation
- tips on how to get a positive mental attitude
- a six-month training plan taking you straight into your first race
- guidance on how to prepare for race day.

So what are you waiting for? Welcome to the world of triathlon.

01

about triathlon

In this chapter you will learn:
- about the early history of triathlon and the Ironman event
- official triathlon distances and points of contact
- the benefits of triathlon.

The early history of triathlon

So how did triathlon start? Contrary to a popular myth, triathlon was not born by the discussions between Navy Captain (now Commander) John Collins and fellow athletes from the Mid-Pacific Road Runners and the Waikiki Swim Club, although this is where the Ironman triathlon came from. The athletes had been discussing who were the fittest, runners or swimmers, during an awards ceremony for the 1977 Perimeter Relay (a running race for five-person teams). They came up with what they thought was the ultimate endurance test combining the three toughest events in Oahu at that time: the 2.4-mile Waikiki Rough Water Swim, the 112-mile Around Oahu bike race and the 26.2-mile Honolulu Marathon.

'Whoever finishes first, we'll call him the Ironman,' Collins said. Of the 15 men to start off the in early morning of 18 February 1978, 12 completed the race and the world's first Ironman, Gordon Haller, won in 11 hours, 46 minutes, 58 seconds. The following year, the first Ironwoman, Lyn Lemaire, a championship cyclist from Boston, placed fifth overall.

Triathlon as a sport actually started four years before in 1974, in Mission Bay in San Diego. The original idea came from Jack Johnstone and Don Shanahan and was sponsored by the San Diego Track Club. In 1973, Jack Johnstone heard about the Dave Pain Birthday swim/run biathlon that was to be held on 28 July that year. The distances were a four-and-a-half mile run followed by a quarter-mile swim. (Most athletes who took part estimated that the actual distance of the swim was around 250 yards rather than the 440 yards advertised). Jack raced in this and subsequent biathlons and enjoyed them, but felt that the swim discipline should be longer to balance the abilities between swimmers and runners.

So, Jack started to organize a biathlon on the Fiesta Island area of Mission Bay where Dave Pain's race had been. After liaising with Don Shanahan, it was decided to put in a bike section as well. The story of triathlon thus started with the Mission Bay triathlon on Wednesday 25 September 1974. The total distances were six miles of running with a longest continuous stretch of 2.8 miles, five miles of cycling, and 500 yards of swimming in two sections of 250 yards. Almost half of the run was barefoot on grass and sand. Forty-six athletes started this first-ever triathlon and Jack Johnstone raced in it as well as organizing it.

The winner was Bill Phillips in 55 minutes and 44 seconds, second was Greg Gillaspie and third Dave Mitchell (Johnstone finished in sixth position). It is important to remember that these were not triathletes. There was no such thing! None of them really trained at anything other than their first sport – either swimming or running, with just a few cyclists; yet without these athletes, triathlon may never have become the sport it is today. Finishing in 35th position was John Collins, who four years later would initiate the Ironman. Other athletes of note who raced in the Mission Bay triathlon in the next few years were Tom Warren who was the winner of the second Ironman competition and two-time Ironman winner, Scott Tinley.

Official and accepted competition distances

In 1989, the International Triathlon Union (ITU) was founded in Avignon, France, on the occasion of the first ever official triathlon World Championships. The official distance for triathlon was set, taken from existing events in each discipline already on the Olympic programme:

* 1500 metre swim
* 40 kilometre cycle
* 10 kilomete run.

This standard distance was used at the Sydney 2000, Athens 2004 and Beijing 2008 Olympic Games, and the Commonwealth Games in Manchester 2002 and Melbourne 2006, and is used for the ITU World Cup series.

Sometimes a relay triathlon will involve three individual athletes taking part in one of the three disciplines and handing over to their teammate for the next discipline. Although triathlon racing can be over any distances, a number of accepted competition distances have developed along with the sport over the years.

Triathlon races	Discipline distances
Supersprint	400 metre swim (1/4 mile) 10 kilometre bike (6 miles) 2 or 3 kilometre run (2 miles)
Sprint	750 metre swim (1/2 mile) 20 kilometre bike (12 miles) 5 kilometre run (3 miles)
Olympic distance	1500 metre swim (1 mile) 40 kilometre bike (25 miles) 10 kilometre run (6 miles)
Half Ironman	1900 metre swim (1.2 miles) 90 kilometre bike (56 miles) 21 kilometre run (13 miles)
Ironman	3800 metre swim (2.4 miles) 180 kilometre bike (112 miles) 42 kilometre run (26.2 miles)

Points of contact

An immediate point of contact is the **British Triathlon Federation,** www.britishtriathlon.org, the governing body of triathlon in Great Britain. British Triathlon can point you in the right direction for a triathlon club, will be able to send you advice on starting training, and can even put you in touch with a triathlon coach or mentor if you want advice. Contacting your local triathlon club means that you'll know when their planned training sessions are and, particularly at the start, it is helpful to have other like-minded people around you who know exactly what you're feeling and what you're going through. In the USA, the best point of contact is www.usatriathlon.org.

They will be able to guide you and help you with any problems – as well as picking you up when things get tough! It's important to make triathlon training enjoyable and part of your life, rather than something that has to be endured. Enjoyment is the crucial factor that will keep you going, and knowing that others are going through the same feelings when training is hard makes it far easier to stick with training and achieve those goals.

The benefits of triathlon

Many newcomers to triathlon are attracted as much for the benefits of health and fitness as for the specific idea of triathlon – the mixture of swimming, cycling, running and general body conditioning.

The benefits of cross training that triathlon offers are immense. Many people come into triathlon as a natural progression from marathon or distance running where the potential for running-related injuries is high. Triathlon offers the opportunity to train as long, or longer than you would for running alone, but with much less chance of injury. There are many other reasons to become involved in triathlons or triathlon training:

- Competing in triathlon can take you all over the world.
- There is less risk of over-use injuries.
- There is less chance of boredom.
- Triathlon uses upper *and* lower body muscles, providing great cross training and overall fitness.
- Mobility and flexibility improve with multi-sport training.
- The 'runner's high', that feeling of euphoria after finishing a long run, will also be duplicated when overcoming the new challenges of training for a triathlon.

Your triathlon training plan – things to consider

Triathlon is a continuous event – you cycle after swimming, and you run after cycling, taking the accumulated fatigue into the next discipline. Because of this, and the different disciplines involved, training for a triathlon requires additional planning. Although all of these points are taken into account in the training sessions and schedules within this book, it's worth just taking some time now to consider some of the following questions. Before doing so you might find it useful to jot down a few things to get you started, namely:

- what your starting level of fitness is, or what sporting background/strengths you might already have
- what discipline you think you'll have to work more at
- things to organize, such as getting a bike or where to swim
- how you plan to fit your training into your week.

General planning and training considerations

What are your strong and weak points?

Which individual sport do you come from?

Do you have experience of racing in another sport?

Have you been to a triathlon event and know what to expect?

What is required to bring you up to a basic level of fitness in your weaker disciplines?

What are your triathlon aims and ambitions?

How hard are you prepared to work to achieve these aims?

How much inconvenience are you prepared to accept?

How much time do you have available to train?

What facilities or coaching do you have available?

With the three individual disciplines of triathlon come additional things to consider:

Swimming

Can you swim? If so, can you swim front crawl?

Do you have access to a swimming pool?

Can you join an adult swimming club? Does it have a teaching group?

Do you panic in open water?

If you are planning to swim in open water, do you own, or can you buy a wetsuit?

Cycling

Can you ride a bike?

Do you possess a bike?

Are you able to do the necessary maintenance to make it safe?

Are you intending to train and race on a bike with dropped handlebars and aerobars, and would you feel competent?

Are you competent cycling on open roads?

Can you practise on quiet roads before going out onto main roads?

Running

Although running is something that everybody can do, you may experience running injuries. Do you have a history of injuries from previous running?

Are you starting triathlon training overweight? If you are, then running can be difficult to begin with, and it might be preferable to do more cycling and swimming until your weight reduces a little.

> **Triathlon training terms**
>
> Training on different sports and different body areas is called 'cross training'. When triathletes train on one sport immediately followed by another sport, it is also called 'back-to-back training' and 'brick training'.

Back-to-back training and brick training

This is the big difference to other sports. Brick training can be very demanding on the body, particularly in the early stages, and there are other things to consider:

- For the start of the cycle discipline you will be sitting on a wet saddle from wearing a swimming costume.
- Your legs will feel weak as blood has pooled in the upper swimming muscles and it takes time for the blood to return to the legs.
- The second transition really brings it home to you what triathlon is about, as your legs, already tired from the cycle discipline, now have to run.

Food and drink

Are you prepared to change your diet? When triathletes are training for many hours each week, they have to eat more than usual in order to give the body enough fuel. New triathletes will often initially lose a significant amount of weight because of the extra training hours they are putting in. The amount and intensity of your training will determine how much extra food is required to maintain your body weight once any excess weight has gone. The type of food you consume will affect how well you train and how you race. Eating a lot of 'junk' food will reduce the effectiveness of your training and your racing.

Juggling: an extra triathlon skill

Most people go to work, have a family, socialize with friends and enjoy a well-rounded lifestyle. Triathlon should be an addition to this rather than taking something away, and that's where the skill of juggling comes in; keeping all the balls in the air at the same time: work, family, friends, a social life and triathlon. It is important to make space for everything. You are not a full-time athlete, but triathlon will be an important part of your life.

Training for a triathlon doesn't need to be all-consuming although you must expect some disruption. Once you've committed yourself to training for and taking part in a triathlon, you've also made that commitment to give up some of your free time, say, approximately six hours a week, for training. Certainly there are many triathletes who do less than this; and there are also the elites, the professionals, who will do six hours each day.

As a new triathlete, you need to decide how you intend to train for your new sport. This book provides an outline of what is required, a logical way of setting about training, and an emphasis on techniques in all disciplines, so that you can prevent yourself from wasting valuable training time and benefit from short cuts that will help you develop more quickly. As you become more experienced and discover the strengths and weaknesses from your individual sport background, in addition to your aptitude for triathlon, you will start taking advice from more experienced triathletes, and have more of an individual perspective of what you require from training and coaching. However, this book is a good starting point and a springboard to move on from.

Training plans are included throughout this book to help prepare you for your first triathlon, but for now, let's take a look at what kit you need to get you started.

02

triathlon clothing and equipment

In this chapter you will learn:
- what to wear – the essentials, the comforts and the luxuries
- about clothing and equipment that will help you train and race more efficiently
- about buying versus borrowing.

To the non-triathlete or newcomer, triathlon might seem an expensive sport with the clothing and equipment from all three disciplines of swimming, cycling and running required in addition to specialist triathlon equipment! What clothing do I wear? What equipment do I use? How much do I have to spend? These questions and many more are answered in this chapter. The good news is that as a novice triathlete, you really don't have to spend too much to begin with. The bad news... triathlon can be addictive, and the pennies in the first year of competition can quickly become pounds and then hundreds as triathlon takes a hold, but this doesn't have to be the case.

Coming into the sport it is very easy to get drawn in and believe that you need to have the best of everything. This simply isn't true. Certainly, it is important to have clothing and equipment that won't let you down, but comfort and convenience are the necessary things. This chapter goes through the three disciplines and looks at **essential** clothing and equipment. You will also read about the extras that will be advantageous, and finally, those luxury items that are available if you want to treat yourself.

Clothing for swimming

The first discipline in almost (but not every) triathlon is the swimming. Many events for novices are pool-based and this is often the sensible way to begin, without the concerns of open water swimming. However, there is no reason not to start with an open water triathlon, particularly if you come from a swimming background and you feel that you are comfortable with the swimming discipline.

Swimming costumes

The first essential is a **costume**, without one of these you won't be allowed in the water! Do buy a decent brand name costume as these will keep their shape and not go loose and floppy after just a couple of training sessions. Zoggs, Speedo and Arena are amongst well-known and reliable swimming names. I'd suggest against buying from a supermarket, as although most costumes may be fine for occasional swimming, training two or three times each week will soon create wear and tear. Expect to pay around £6–£10 for a man's pair of trunks and from £10–£20 for a women's costume. I have always been happy buying swimming clothing and equipment from www.swimshop.co.uk.

> **Top tip**
>
> Specialist swimmers will often have different-sized costumes for
> training and racing. There are two reasons for this; the extra drag
> in larger costumes used in training will make them feel fast when
> they put on a smaller costume and step onto the blocks for
> racing, and also the tightness of a racing costume will make the
> swimmer more hydrodynamic.

Many swimmers will also have a pair of 'drag' swimming trunks
for training. For triathletes, drag costumes can simulate to a
certain extent the drag that might be felt in an open water swim.
These drag trunks are worn over the normal costume (women
wear a pair of trunks over their normal swimming costume, men
the larger drag trunks over their ordinary training trunks), and
create extra resistance during swim training.

However, don't be tempted to buy a costume that is too small
because it will ride up your backside throughout the race and
will be extremely uncomfortable. Also avoid the temptation to
buy an expensive costume that is advertised as a 'racing'
costume. These are unlikely to last a long time. For you, fit and
comfort are the essentials.

Tri-suits

These are all-in-one suits (think of a women's swimming costume
with short legs, similar to cycling shorts), and are often worn for
racing and some training. It is a personal choice whether you
choose a tri-suit – some triathletes feel more comfortable in
them, whilst others wear a swimming costume for all three
disciplines when racing. A tri-suit will cost from £30.

> **Dress for a quick transition**
>
> Wearing the same race clothing for all three disciplines is one of
> the aspects of triathlon that people seeing the sport from the
> outside find quite incredible! But, think about it, if you wear the
> same clothes for all three disciplines and minimize time in the
> transition area, you will be that much faster. This is one of the
> reasons that triathletes choose not to wear socks; it takes time to
> put them on.

Wetsuits

Wetsuits are not only an option; below a certain water temperature they become compulsory, and are allowed to be worn by age-groupers (the non-elite triathletes) up to a water temperature of 24°C. Wetsuits are made of neoprene rubber and are allowed to be a maximum of five millimetres thick. They aren't cheap! Good suits will start from around £150. It is absolutely essential that you get a swimming-specific, correct-fitting wetsuit. Go to a triathlon specialist shop and also take advice from more experienced triathletes.

Wetsuit advantage

Seasoned triathletes call the wetsuit the 'equalizer' as it can make the difference in performance between the good and the average, or between the average and poor swimmer. This is due to:

- the added buoyancy provided by the neoprene
- the more streamlined flat position
- the added confidence of wearing one.

Wetsuits designed for sailing, surfing or diving will inhibit a smooth swimming action and stroke. Even with a triathlon wetsuit, you must have the correct size. If it is too small you will be extremely uncomfortable. Tightness around the chest will restrict breathing and make the arm action uncomfortable. If it is too big, you will negate any advantages, as the suit will allow too much water in and create drag in the water. It's good to allow a little water in as this will heat up with your body temperature and keep you warm, making the wetsuit do its job.

Equipment for swimming

Swimming goggles

The next essential is a pair of swimming **goggles**. Again, buy a reputable brand and make sure that:

- the goggles fit comfortably
- the goggles don't leak
- the goggles don't mist up.

It might be difficult to test for these points in a shop, but you should certainly test your goggles during training to make sure they are good for racing. A good pair of goggles will not normally mist up, but in very warm and very cold conditions this can happen, particularly when the outside temperature is very different from the temperature of your face! Also, as goggles get older they are more likely to start misting up.

Top tip

Buy an anti-mist solution and put a couple of drops on the inside of your goggles to prevent misting.

It is, of course, essential that you keep your goggles clean; a couple of drops of washing-up liquid every two months will help with this but you must rinse it out properly. Without goggles you will have permanently sore eyes from swimming in a chlorine-treated swimming pool, and when you are racing in open water and swimming in a pack of triathletes, being able to see what's going on has several benefits:

- It will help you to swim straight.
- It allows you to follow a swimmer (see drafting section in Chapter 05).
- It can be the difference between getting stuck behind the pack or being handily placed in or near the lead.

Many triathletes wear **contact lenses** and will want to race in them as well. This is no problem but it's vital that your goggles don't leak. It is also possible to buy prescription goggles. The cost for a reliable pair of non-prescription goggles will start at around £3 and go up to £15. As with the swimming costume, don't be tempted to buy the latest goggles that are advertised to do everything for you: fit and comfort are the essentials.

Swimming hats

If you have long hair, a **swimming hat** can lower water resistance and save you time. The cost for a swim hat is low unless you want to buy a neoprene hat (this will help prevent heat loss) or a slightly insulated hat, when the cost can go up to £6. Many triathlon event organizers supply a swimming hat to race in.

Water bottles

Don't forget a non-glass **water bottle**, you'll need it for every
training session, particularly for the swim sessions when you
don't always realize that you're sweating and you can easily
become dehydrated. Cost for a water bottle is minimal, perhaps
£1, and many race organizers will offer a water bottle in the
race pack.

Fins

Fins (often wrongly called flippers) are a necessity if you are a
weak swimmer. They are a fantastic aid when you are learning
to get the correct flat body position (this is discussed further in
Chapter 04), although you can't use them in a race of course!
Don't buy the overlong fins that are used by scuba divers and
snorkellers, buy shorter, specialized **swimming fins**, and expect
to pay around £10 to £15 for a good pair.

A **pull buoy** and **kickboard** are also welcome additions, costing
between £5 to £10 each. A kickboard is held in front of the
body to work on kicking technique, and using a pull buoy can
help to simulate the slightly different position resulting from
wearing a wetsuit during a race – due to the added buoyancy
from the neoprene. During training, place the pull buoy between
the tops of your legs and squeeze to keep it in place.

Clothing for cycling

Cycling is usually the second discipline in a triathlon. It is the longest section of the race, and the greatest improvements in performance, certainly in the early stages, can be made here.

Crash hats

A crash hat is the single most important item that you'll buy; it might even save your life (mine certainly did and a most fetching scar on my elbow is a constant reminder to what might have been). Don't make false economies here; expect to pay £30 or more for a legal, safe crash hat. If you are unlucky enough to have a crash, particularly if the hat hits a solid surface, you **must** buy a new one afterwards. Using a crash hat that may have been damaged or a second-hand one whose history you don't know is not only a false economy, it is potentially life-threatening.

Cycling shoes

These may be seen as a luxury if you're just starting out, and there is certainly nothing wrong in using running or training shoes for your first few events. You may even save a few seconds in transitions as you won't need to change shoes between cycling and running. However, cycling shoes do give you an advantage as they attach to the pedals, giving you better cycling stability and power. For those people who prefer to cycle wearing running shoes or trainers, there is an attachment called **Thompson pedals adaptors**. These are basically a flat lightweight metal surface that fits into or onto pedals and give a solid base for the shoes to rest on. These are relatively expensive, starting at £40.

If you're borrowing a bike, you may well be able to persuade your lender to donate their cycling shoes (assuming the size/fit is the same). If you can't persuade them, then the cycle shoes are going to cost you at least £50. You will also need to make sure that the cycle shoes and **cycle pedals** are compatible.

Cycle shorts

Cycle shorts might seem to be one item that you'd prefer to buy (expect £20 and upwards) rather than borrow, but there's nothing wrong with borrowing a used but clean pair of shorts. Make sure the **chamois** ('chammy') or similar insert is clean and has a lot of wear left in it. The chammy is the padded section inside the shorts that gives some comfort from a long ride in the saddle.

Cycle singlets and jerseys

You don't need a purpose-made **tri-suit** to compete in, but something close-fitting and comfortable and – if you are taking part in an open water swim – something that can be worn under a wetsuit is ideal. A singlet and shorts will serve you just as well, but extra padding in the saddle area is desirable. Cycle jerseys cost around £10 or more. They are close-fitting and will make you feel good in training; they also have back pockets to carry food.

Socks and gloves

While you probably won't want to waste time by putting on **socks** after the swim for cycle racing, the comfort for training makes them worthwhile. However, do ride and run a few times without socks before your first event so that you won't blister or chaff during the race. Cycle gloves also add comfort on long or cold rides.

Turbo wind trainers

A real luxury? Get yourself a **turbo (wind) trainer** (more on this in Chapter 06). Some prices can be in the exotic range… but a more than competent model can be bought for around £40. A turbo trainer is a mechanical aid that you can fit your bike onto for indoor training. It has a roller at the back and the bike is held by clips on the axle of the rear wheel off the floor; it's similar to a fixed bicycle in a gym, but has the added benefit of you being able to train on your own bike rather than one that might not suit you or your riding position. However, there is nothing wrong with using a gym bike if you don't have a turbo trainer. It makes sense to be able to do the quality cycle sessions without worrying about traffic conditions and avoiding the worst of the British weather.

Equipment for cycling

Bikes

You have to have a **bike**. It is an essential piece of triathlon
equipment. However, new bikes can be extremely expensive,
and if you decide later not to carry on in triathlon, you will have
paid out a lot of money. It is certainly not unusual to see bikes
advertised for £2000 or even more. The most important piece of
cycling equipment…? Your legs! However good a bike you may
buy, without the appropriate training to get strong legs, you
won't be taking advantage of it.

Many newcomers to the sport begin using a mountain bike,
although you will soon notice that racing (road) bikes are much
lighter and faster. Initially, don't worry about buying an
expensive bike – there are other options available:

- Use your own old bike that's been sitting in the garage. If you
  do, give it a good service – faulty equipment or punctures will
  not only lead to the end of a training session or race but could
  also mean serious injury).
- Borrow a bike from a triathlete or cycling friend.
- Buy a second-hand bike.
- Consider using a mountain bike for your first event and
  training on it for that event.

Second-hand bikes

There are always good quality second-hand bikes on sale from
perhaps £300 in magazines such as *Cycling Weekly* and 220
triathlon, and on many triathlon websites. Take advice from an
experienced cyclist or triathlete, particularly about the correct-
sized bike. You will find more information on this in Chapter 06.

Puncture repair kits

You'll also need a **puncture repair outfit**; you won't be able to
borrow one of these because sensible cyclists and triathletes
always carry theirs with them. Around £5 or less will buy you
one that will get you home if you are unlucky enough to
puncture. Punctures are always a worry for new cyclists and
new triathletes. It is well worthwhile taking advice from an

experienced athlete as to exactly how to mend a puncture and, perhaps more importantly for a race, how to change an inner tube. An extra **inner tube** or tubular tyre ('tub') is always useful so that you can change the puncture by the roadside and repair when you get home.

Dealing with a puncture

If you have a puncture during a race, your chances of winning are very low! Having a puncture can be totally frustrating, however it should be easy to fix.

Initially, if you are not used to fixing punctures it can take some time, but it does get easier with practice. It is generally faster to replace the inner tube with a spare rather than try to patch a tube that is on the bike, particularly as puncture glue takes at least five minutes to dry properly.

If you get a puncture, first check the tyre to see if you can find anything that may have caused the puncture. If it is obvious, then you may be able to pull out that section of the tube and patch the spot without removing the wheel and then the tube. If you cannot find what caused the puncture remove the inner tube, inflate it and listen, or feel, for escaping air. When you have found out where the air is coming from, check that section of tyre for glass or other sharp objects and remove them. Do be careful, as there is no point in replacing an inner tube only for it to be punctured again. Many people choose to use puncture resistant tyres, which have protective strips of materials such as Kevlar inside them.

Removing the inner tube

Remove the wheel, undo the valve cap, remove the threaded metal collar (if there is one), empty any air out of the tube and push the valve back into the rim.

Fit two or three tyre levers into the rim about two centimetres apart and pull them back, levering one side of the tyre out and over the side of the rim. Be careful that you are not pinching the tube while you lever the tyre out. Remove the middle one of the three levers, and hook it under the tyre about two centimetres past one of the other two. You then have three levers in place again, but a longer section of the tyre is hooked over the rim. Take the middle lever out and repeat the process again. When a third of the tyre is hooked over the rim, the rest will come off more easily.

The tyre should stay on one side of the rim. Hold the inner tube at the valve hole, push the valve up through the rim and pull the valve out from the tyre. Pull the rest of the inner tube out.

Mending the puncture

To find the hole you can either pump the tube up and feel/listen for the air coming out or hold the tube under water and see where bubbles appear. Then, deflate the tyre, clean the area around the hole and make sure it is dry. Use sandpaper to rub around the puncture hole, and mark the hole with a ballpoint pen or chalk.

Apply rubber solution until you have an area slightly larger than the patch, keeping the hole in the middle all the time. Let the rubber solution dry (five minutes) but don't let any dirt stick to it.

Peel off the backing paper/foil/plastic on one side of the patch and be careful not to get dirt or fingerprints on the patch itself. Place it on the inner tube so that the middle of the patch covers the hole, and make sure that the patch is in contact with the rubber solution all around the edge. Squeeze the patch hard into the rubber solution for about a minute.

To remove the backing paper on the patch, fold the inner tube in half so that the backing paper on the patch splits down the middle. Carefully peel the backing off from the middle towards the edge to avoid lifting the edge of the patch.

Dust the top of the patch and any exposed areas of rubber solution with chalk/talc to stop it sticking inside the tyre.

Finally, give the inner tube two or three strokes of the pump before putting it back on the wheel. This prevents the tube getting pinched when you put the tyre back on.

Replacing the inner tube

Starting at the valve hole, put the inner tube onto the rim under the tyre. Then hook the tyre back onto the rim with your hands, making sure that the inner tube does not get pinched, and that the tyre is seated properly on the rim. You may need to use a tyre lever to get the last section of tyre back on the rim. Replace the threaded collar, pump up the tyre and replace the dust cap.

Top tip

Always carry an extra inner tube with you on the bike, both in training and racing. It is much quicker to change an inner tube than to mend a puncture. You can then mend the puncture at home when it is more convenient. Having a puncture during training is inconvenient, but knowing how to change the inner tube during a race situation can save many minutes and ensure that you are still able to finish the race.

Clothing for running

The final discipline in a triathlon requires at least one essential:

Running shoes

You must buy **running shoes**.

Every individual has their own way of running and this will have an impact on how the shoes wear. Don't borrow running shoes (except in an emergency) – this can lead to you getting injured. I would suggest that if you are a new runner, don't buy **light racing flats** (these are specialist, very lightweight racing shoes worn by accomplished runners). Instead, use your own trainers for your first race. These will be more cushioned and comfortable than racing flats and are less likely to cause injury.

Never buy mail order or by the internet. Go into a good running or triathlon shop and be advised by good staff. Expect to pay £40 or more to begin with. You'll be allowed to try them on and even jog around the shop.

Top tip

Time-saving devices – another valuable investment is in a pair of **lace locks**. Similar to the locks used on tents, they allow the laces to go inside the lock and can be quickly pulled tight to do the laces up, saving you a few seconds during transition. An alternative would be elastic laces for the shoes or a **Velcro shoelace**. These all cost £1 to £2.

Running shorts

Even if you choose to race in a tri-suit or swimming costume, you might want **running shorts** to put over the top for cycling and/or running. Get the correct size and make sure they don't have raised seams or edges which will chafe or cut into your inside thighs and ensure that you're not able to train for several days. Expect to pay from £5.

Running tops

Any comfortable **vest or T-shirt** is fine for training and also for racing in your first event.

Added extras

You might also want to buy a **peaked hat** and **sunglasses** as protection from sunny weather. At the other extreme, a woolly hat and running tights along with a sweatshirt or tracksuit might be worthwhile for those winter training days.

Equipment for running

Other things to consider buying are a **heart rate monitor (HRM)** and a **training diary**. A HRM is worn on your wrist, similar to a watch with a sensor on a strap around your chest. The sensor picks up the heart rate and feeds it to the display on your wrist. It will give you instant feedback on your training (heart rate, time, distance, etc.), but be warned, it is not an instant panacea and heart rates can be affected by several things including illness and overtraining, as well as training exertion. HRMs are now excellent value and entry-level monitors can be as little as £15.

Most triathletes keep **training diaries,** but how many use them properly? For many, it is merely a book to record the training done. For the intelligent diary keeper, it's a record of what sessions preceded the best race and which sessions were immediately before a poor race; an indication of what works best in training.

Essentials, maybes and extravagant extras

Starting out in triathlon really doesn't need to cost that much if you plan it properly and don't become an 'all-the-gear-and-no-idea' first-timer. The truth is, you can get away with very little at entry level, and many people spend far too much because they think that they have to. Frankly, you don't! Triathlon equipment costs can be pretty reasonable, but professional gear will add up at an astounding rate.

Here's a reminder of the essentials, maybes and extravagant extras for each of the three disciplines: the swim, the cycle and the run.

Essentials	Maybes	Extravagant extras
Costume	Swim hat	Wetsuit
Goggles	Tri-suit	Pull buoy
Water bottle		Kickboard
Fins		Drag trunks
Bike	Cycle jersey	Mitts/gloves
Crash hat	Extra tyres	Turbo wind trainer
Cycle shoes	Extra inner tubes	Thompson pedals
Cycle shorts	Socks	
Puncture repair kit	Sunglasses	
Water bottle		
Running shoes	Socks	Tights
Running shorts	Sunglasses	Woolly hat
Vest/T-shirt	Peaked hat	
Water bottle	Lace locks	
	Rain jacket	

Top tips

When getting your triathlon clothing and equipment consider these points:

- Take advice from experienced triathletes.
- Consider borrowing or buying second-hand to start with.
- Don't always buy top of the range.
- Whatever it is... make sure it fits!
- Don't skimp on shoes, goggles or a swim costume, and run/cycle shorts; you'll appreciate the comfort!

Now you've got the kit, it's time to plan your triathlon training schedule.

03

how to get the most out of your triathlon training

In this chapter you will learn:
- how to fit training into your life
- the general principles of training
- about core conditioning
- about triathlon training periodization.

Getting started in any new sport is a challenge, but getting started in triathlon with its different disciplines is even more challenging! How on earth do you start training for a triathlon? When you're first starting out, you might be considering questions like:

Which discipline is most important?

Should I swim, cycle and run on the same day or on different days?

How can I fit it all in?

How many hours a week is reasonable?

How hard should I be training to get results?

Later on in this book you will learn all about swimming training, cycle training and running training, but before that, this chapter provides an overview of things to consider before you start your triathlon training. When combining training sessions for three different disciplines done back-to-back, it is important to understand the basic principles of training so that you can achieve maximum results in minimum time without overtraining.

As well as planning a basic triathlon training schedule and looking at triathlon periodization throughout the year, we will be discussing aspects of exercise physiology such as:

- training overload
- specificity
- rest and recovery
- overtraining and how to avoid it.

Although these principles have been applied to the training sessions throughout this book, understanding these principles will ensure that you get the most out of your triathlon training and enable you to plan your own training sessions.

Fitting training in

It is absolutely crucial that triathlon doesn't take over your life to the detriment of a balanced lifestyle. The secret of enjoyment and ensuring that triathlon is part of your life for a long time to come is to slot the training into everyday life. Most of us work around eight hours each day, five days each week. We all have other commitments apart from work: family and social commitments, all the things that go to making life worthwhile. Evenings during the week are precious, and although training can and should be a social occasion as well, it's important to have some non-training time to be able to spend with your family and non-triathlete friends.

Finding time slots

There are a number of time slots that we can use for training:

- early morning before work
- lunchtimes
- early evening after work
- later evenings
- weekends
- extra bonus 'wasted' time – the commute to and from work.

Making the most of dead time

If your workplace is within reasonable running or cycling distance then use that journey to and from work on some occasions each week to serve a two-fold purpose – it will save you time and money! Using journey time for training does mean that you have to be organized, probably taking in several changes of clothing on Monday morning and bringing home that same clothing at the end of the week on a Friday evening. In theory, doing this creates ten extra training times. In practice, this might be three or four training sessions, but that is certainly an appropriate way of making best use of time available during the week.

Many swimming clubs, triathlon clubs and local authority swimming pools have early-morning swimming sessions for adults from as early as 6.00 a.m., so if you schedule in perhaps two sessions here per week, that frees up a further amount of evening time. Add in a couple of lunchtime sessions for swimming, running, gym work (weights, core conditioning or an exercise bike session), and you are well over halfway to ensuring that your valuable free time is still available to you. Weekends can be used for one long running session and one long cycle, and by careful time management you will still have the majority of your evenings free.

Sample weekly training schedule

MONDAY	a.m. Take clothes into work lunch Swim p.m. Commute – run home
TUESDAY	6.00 a.m. Swim a.m. Commute cycle to work p.m. Commute cycle home
WEDNESDAY	REST
THURSDAY	6.00 a.m. Swim a.m. Commute cycle to work p.m. Commute cycle home
FRIDAY	a.m. Commute run to work p.m. Take clothes home from work
SATURDAY	a.m. Long easy run with club
SUNDAY	a.m. Long easy cycle with club

Now this is only an example of what is possible, and you must work out what is good for you. However, this particular week's schedule has three swims, three runs, and five cycle rides – all this without having to take out even one evening from your social life! Juggling and time managing really is an essential triathlon skill!

Of course many people do not have the luxury of being able to use the commute to and from work as training time, and this is when it becomes even more important to arrange your training times carefully and give yourself at least a couple of evenings at home or free to follow other activities. You may well feel that the above is too demanding in terms of time, and if you are coming from a relatively sedentary lifestyle, it would be better to have no more than one training session per day, on perhaps as few as three days each week to begin with, gradually increasing sessions as your body adapts to the training. Any guidelines for the newcomer are just that, guidelines, and individuals adapt differently to the training stimulus.

> **Top tip**
>
> What I would suggest is 'make haste slowly'; don't try to do too much too quickly, and when you do add on extra hours or extra sessions, do it gradually. If you start with three hours of training each week, add no more than half an hour every three weeks. Even with this, at the end of just three months, you will be up to five hours per week and importantly, you will be unlikely to have suffered any overuse or muscular injuries.

Before we look at any type of training in detail, let's consider the energy systems you use, and the general principles of training.

The energy systems

You should be aware of (or at least have an idea of) the energy systems that are used during racing and training. The intensity and duration of each training session or race determines which energy system you use, although more than one system is usually in use at any one time.

- Lower intensity, longer duration exercise tends to use the aerobic system, utilizing carbohydrate and fat for energy.
- Higher intensity, shorter duration tends to use the anaerobic system, utilizing purely carbohydrate for energy (more about this later in Chapter 10).

The aerobic system (with oxygen)

Aerobic training develops the cardiovascular system (heart and lungs), improving your cardiovascular fitness level. This is an essential need for you as a triathlete as it creates the ability to keep going for a long time. If you are doing exercise that you can continue with for more than a few minutes you are using this system – particularly during lower intensity, longer duration exercise sessions. Steady long runs, swims and rides will use the aerobic system as will low intensity, interval type training.

The anaerobic system (without oxygen)

Exercising and training at a higher intensity when we can't feed the muscles with the oxygen they need is anaerobic training.

When you see athletes collapsing immediately after a race, it is because they have run, swim or cycled anaerobically, and their bodies, hearts and lungs are screaming out to get some oxygen back in their bodies. The anaerobic system produces a waste product called **lactic acid** which contributes to muscle fatigue. This is converted into lactate and removed from the muscles via the circulation. A good warm-down, which enhances elevated circulation without taxing the muscles too much, helps to remove the lactic acid. The anaerobic system is used for medium and high intensity training; interval and repetition training, power and speed training.

The principles of training

As the three elements of triathlon combined (or individually in longer events) cover fairly long distances, triathlon is an endurance event. One of the most daunting things when you begin training for a triathlon is to figure out exactly *how* you train for triathlon. If you were embarking upon just one sport, swimming, cycling *or* running, then there would be tried-and-tested methods and principles of training to follow. With triathlon, there are still those principles, but you have to consider all three disciplines, and crucially, the interaction between them.

If you attempted to combine the normal weekly training schedules for swimming, cycling and running into one week, it is more than likely that a breakdown from overuse injuries would occur. There is a need to combine these three training regimes, but not at the expense of injury. The good news about triathlon training is that working on the three disciplines is **complementary**. Swimming is largely upper body based while cycling and running are legs based. The likelihood is for fewer injuries to be sustained training for a triathlon than training on an individual sport.

There are different ways of training and the general types of training used in triathlon can be summarized as follows. All of these types of training are incorporated into the training sessions in this book.

Endurance training	To improve cardiovascular fitness and train the energy systems and muscles needed for endurance events.
Race pace (tempo)	Higher intensity training to get you up to race speed.
Interval training	Used to progress training to the next level.
Power and strength (hills, resistance)	Higher intensity training to strengthen muscles or replicate race conditions.
Technique	Drills and skills to fine-tune technique, making you faster and better.
Mental toughness	Incorporated in most endurance and high intensity training sessions – if the mind is tough, the body will follow!

This is, of course, a gross oversimplification. However, within these compartments most areas of training can be included. Detailed training sessions for swimming, cycling and running are included in the chapters following this one, and they all include all of these types of training.

Endurance and strength

It is essential to work on endurance, strength, power and speed so that you can excel in each of these disciplines. Muscular endurance is the ability of the muscle to perform repetitive contractions (to keep going) over a long period of time. Muscular strength is the development of maximum force in a muscle or group of muscles. This is important in triathlon if you have an upper body weakness (swimming), leg weakness (cycling and also running), or central core weakness (stomach and pelvic support muscles) which can affect any discipline. Exercises for the core (abdominal) muscles are included at the end of this chapter.

Overload

Overload means that when your body has achieved one level of fitness with one level of training, a greater overload has to be applied in the next level of training to create further progression. In other words, you have to keep working harder to get progressively better. So, the level of training is made more demanding until the body adapts to this, and then a new, harder level of training begins, and so on. Overload can be achieved through changing many different elements of training:

- increasing duration on any or all disciplines (training for longer)
- increasing speed on any or all disciplines (going faster)
- increasing intensity on any or all disciplines (hills, resistance)
- improving or changing technique (this makes it harder)
- reducing rest or recovery time.

These increasing demands take place over a long period of time, years in many cases, rather than an increase in demand in every single training session. Overloading in training will eventually force the body to change. The initial response is tiredness and fatigue, creating the need for recovery, but this recovery and adaptation will gradually lift your fitness levels higher and higher.

When you begin training, it is very difficult to imagine where training can lead to. It is difficult to imagine the level of fitness that can be achieved over one or two years. Therefore, when you plan your training sessions it is important that there is a foreseeable and realistic time when improvements can be assessed. If the training load is too little, there is little or no increase in fitness level and performance. If the training load is too stressful, your body will not adapt and you may get injured or become ill.

All your training sessions must take into account the following in all three disciplines of swimming, cycling and running:

- how often (frequency) you train
- how long (duration) you train for
- how much (amount) work you will do in a training session
- how hard (intensity) the session is going to be.

There is stress and fatigue from working out in three disciplines that may not be immediately noticed. If this extra stress is not seen and dealt with, it will lead to burn out and lack of results.

To begin with, start slowly – it is better to do too little rather than too much.

Stress – good or bad?

All demands on the mind or body are stress. Good (positive) stress that the body can deal with and adapt to is called **eustress**, and bad (negative) stress that the body is unable to deal with is called **distress**. In terms of training, the correct level is eustress.

To gain maximum training benefits we have to place the body under enough stress so that it creates a training effect and adapts, rather than overtraining and putting the body in distress. It is necessary for training to be pitched at the correct level for adaptation to occur, and can be difficult to find the fine line between stress and distress.

Adaptation

This is how your body changes, gets used to, and adapts to training. Adaptation is the change that happens to your body when new stresses are put upon it. Training for triathlon is how you improve your fitness in order to improve your performance. You should always look at training as **long term** rather than **short term**. It is essential that the demands are progressive and that they are specific to you and your level of fitness. Any training has to be specific to the sport, and for triathlon that means not only specific to swimming, cycling and running, but also to the demands of the crossover effect of the continuous endurance as one discipline follows another.

The bigger picture

Many people don't understand that the body becomes stronger and fitter not just through training, but also through the rest and recovery afterwards. Training is a continuous process of:

- effort that tires and breaks down the body
- recovery from these efforts
- super-compensation and adaptation to these demands.

Without enough recovery from training efforts, your body will always be in a state of fatigue and not able to perform to its potential. This is why we taper (reduce) training prior to a race (see Chapter 11). Stressful training damages the cells in the body, and after a training session the body is weaker, not stronger. The extent of the weakness and damage will depend on the duration, amount and intensity of training. After training, with the correct recovery, rest, and refuelling with food and water, your body will adapt and adjust, and in this way prepare itself for more, and harder, training.

Specificity

The specificity of exercise in any sport produces its own specific response and adaptations. You must bear this in mind if and when you train with other athletes. In other words:

- Swimming will get you swimming-fit.
- Cycling will get you cycling-fit.
- Running will get you running-fit.
- Practising the changeover from swim to cycle, and from cycle to run will improve how your body copes with this.
- Practising transition will improve your transition.

Training in each of the disciplines will lead to improvements in that discipline, although there is likely to be some fitness benefits, particularly if your general fitness level is fairly low to begin with. In the early days, building up a good aerobic level of fitness gives a good grounding for the endurance requirements of triathlon.

Individuality

The first essential of training and the most important, is that every athlete – including you – is an individual. Whatever accepted knowledge there is on any sport, it may not necessarily be correct for every individual. You will respond in your own individual way to training with your unique genetic make-up, individual anatomy (how your body is built) and physiology (how your body works). These will affect your responses to training, as will your sporting or non-sporting background and your strengths and weaknesses. Ask yourself if there is a need to play 'catch-up' on one (perhaps two) particular discipline(s) and back off from the strong one.

It is necessary to look at where you're coming from, and where you want to go to. In addition to this, you should consider the following points:

- Your level of fitness coming into triathlon will affect the appropriate level of training.
- Your age is a factor as well. Two people of the same age may easily be at very different levels of maturity and biological age depending on previous activities.
- It is also important to assess how much sleep and rest you need.
- You need to understand how much recovery time you need from stressful training sessions.
- How does your body react to hot and cold weather? Do you need a long warm-up in colder weather to prevent injury?
- Have you had any previous serious or debilitating illnesses that need to be taken into account?

It is vitally important for you to be aware of your current fitness level – it is very easy to fall into the trap of remembering a fitness level and amount of training undertaken a number of years previously when, perhaps, you were in a totally different state of fitness. Don't assume that you can re-start at that level. Comparisons between 'now' and 'then' are both unfair and unhelpful to you.

Technique

The importance of a good technique in all three disciplines cannot be overemphasized. You should always try to work on excellent technique throughout. Drills and skills to work on technique are given in the following chapters on swimming, cycling and running.

Reversibility

If you stop training, the improvements in performance also stop and will eventually reverse – you will lose your fitness. How much will depend on you as an individual. Very roughly, any improvements in level of fitness are lost in approximately half the time at which they were gained. However, there is a cumulative effect, and if you have trained for several years, you will tend to lose fitness more slowly than people who have been training for only a very short time.

Holding a level of fitness

Fitness will not evaporate immediately even without hard training. If you are doing a lot of races during the summer, it is a good idea to taper (reduce) your training to accommodate the races. Training sensibly while racing will maintain your overall fitness.

Overtraining

Attempting to do too much too soon is often the cause of injury. There is a natural tendency to want to improve quickly, but overtraining can and will lead to injuries. Overtraining occurs when you continuously increase the training load without giving yourself time to adapt or recover.

Signs of overtraining include:

- reduced performance in training and racing despite hard training
- constant tiredness
- irritability and moodiness
- getting upset at small things
- sleeping too much or too little, or finding it difficult to sleep
- a loss of appetite or eating inappropriately (binge eating)
- no motivation for training or racing
- persistent muscle soreness
- constant colds or a runny nose
- recurring minor illness or niggling injury.

The solution is to rest until you feel completely recovered.

Your heart, lungs and muscles do adapt to training, but it takes a little longer for your tendons and ligaments. As the training load increases, tendons and ligaments do not develop as quickly as muscles and can become stressed. The first stage of overuse is inflammation and tendinopathy. This is relatively easy to deal with, although it is essential to reduce the amount of training to make a full recovery quickly. A poor technique may also lead to injury as the constant repetition of an inefficient action uses the muscles in an incorrect way.

Avoiding overtraining

It is important to have easy or rest days each week, and easy or rest weeks in each phase (say, four to six weeks) of training. The amount of training (the training load) should only be increased very gradually over a period of time, no more than 15 per cent over a six-week period. Training load can apply to any of the following; it's important not to change too much in one go, but to plan a step-by-step approach, so you would only plan to change one or two of these elements in any one training session:

- duration
- intensity
- power
- strength
- technique
- endurance.

Stretching and flexibility will help recovery and therefore avoid the pitfalls of overtraining. An appropriate warm-up and warm-down will help avoid injury, as will massage. If you have previously had injuries, be aware of what caused them.

Rest and recovery

As we have seen earlier, recovery is the most important part of the training programme because adaptation takes place during this recovery. Don't ignore this and do take adequate rest. If you don't, you will not make the improvements that you could and may also suffer from injury and illness.

For most triathletes, the weight-bearing nature of running makes it more stressful than cycling and swimming. Anaerobic (high intensity) training tends to be more stressful than aerobic training and requires more recovery. Remember this when planning your training programme.

Core conditioning

There is no doubt that triathlon is a time-consuming sport, and there is often little time to do the extras that may form part of the triathlon training programme such as weight training, stretching and flexibility. However, I would suggest that there is one addition that will pay dividends: working on your core muscles. Training these muscles has several benefits:

- Well-conditioned core stabilizing muscles contribute to better technique during swimming, cycling and running.
- Stronger core muscles reduce the risk of injury in other muscle groups.
- It also ensures that the extra fatigue that sets in after the transition changes from swimming to cycling and from cycling to running is manageable, and that you will still be able to race well despite that fatigue.

There are many different ways of working on and exercising the core muscles – to cover them all would take a book in itself. However, the following sets of exercises will make a big difference to your training, posture, technique and racing, particularly if you haven't done them before. I would go as far as to say that athletes, and triathletes particularly, are unlikely to make the best use of their abilities if they do not use core stability as an integral part of their training schedule.

Basic balances

These balances are a type of functional exercise, and an enormous aid to core stability. Each position should be held for ten seconds to start with, gradually working up by five-second increments to a maximum of 30–60 seconds. Once this has been established, a series of abdominal exercises should be added between each balance position. My suggestion would be to start with ten repetitions and increase the number of repetitions to fill 30 seconds. I have had a number of athletes work for as long as 90 seconds on the abdominal exercises but they did start with ten reps and work up gradually.

1. The plank

You begin in the classic press-up position with both arms and feet supporting the body.

figure 3.1 the plank position

Aim to create a straight line along the body from head to feet (like a plank) and maintain this position... basically, don't drop the hips!

- Arms should be held shoulder width apart, elbows unlocked.
- Feet should also be parted about the same distance as the arms.
- Feet should be balanced on toes with toes pushing downwards directly below heels and not with heels either facing inwards or outwards.
- Hold abdominal muscles in tightly (this is most important – if you fail to do this, the lower back will take all the strain).
- Keep breathing throughout.
- Try to hold for ten seconds or longer as you progress.

2. The plank on elbows

This is the same exercise but performed with bent arms, resting on the elbows and toes. This alternative is for athletes who do not have enough basic body strength or balance to begin with.

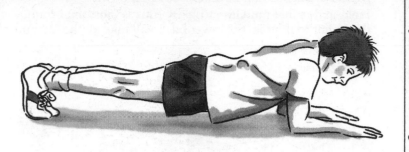

figure 3.2 the plank position on elbows

Body weight can also be taken on the knees rather than the toes if necessary, although it shouldn't be necessary to do the basic starting position on both knees **and** elbows. The exercise tips for the plank on elbows and knees remain the same.

figure 3.3 the plank position on elbows and knees

3. The plank with arm and leg raises

The next four positions consist of lifting and raising individually and in turn, each leg and each arm. This works the core muscles as they contract to maintain balance. It is essential to maintain that straight line along the long axis from head to feet and not drop the hips throughout these balance exercises. As you do each exercise, remember the following:

- Maintain the position of other body parts.
- Hold abdominal muscles in tightly (this is most important – if you fail to do this, the lower back will take all the strain).
- Keep breathing throughout.

Single leg raise

figure 3.4 single leg raise in the plank position

- The foot and leg should be lifted with the foot at or just below hip level.
- Keep the hips in a straight line, with the hip bones facing the floor – use a mirror, friend or coach to ensure that your hips remain level.
- Alternate legs.
- Ensure all movements are slow and controlled.

Single arm raise

- Alternate arms are lifted so they are parallel to the floor and pointing directly ahead.
- Ensure that you keep the body in a straight line, making sure that you do not lift the hip and shoulder on the side that the arm is raised, rotating the body – keep the body facing the floor.
- Keep the hips in a straight line, with the hip bones facing the floor - use a mirror, friend or coach to ensure that your hips remain level.
- Alternate arms.
- Ensure all movements are slow and controlled.

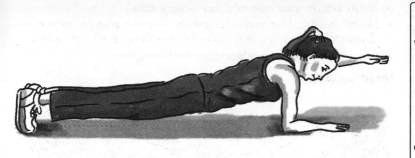

figure 3.5 single arm raise in the plank position

Alternate arm and leg raise

figure 3.6 alternate arm and leg raise in the plank position

The usual response and reaction to this is to feel completely unstable. The hips will move up and down to react to the feeling of instability. This is completely natural and is, of course, where the need for core stability comes in. Do persevere with this and the next balance position as they are the first of the more difficult ones and give tremendous improvements in core stability.

• An alternate arm and leg are lifted (e.g. left arm and right leg simultaneously, or right arm and left leg).
• The leg should be at hip height, the arm at shoulder height.

- Ensure that you keep the body in a straight line facing the floor.
- Alternate sides.
- Ensure all movements are slow and controlled.

Star balances

The balance is moved away from the basic starting position and taken onto your side, so the outside of the right foot and the right hand are in contact with the floor (and then the outside of the left foot is coupled with the left hand). The supporting arm should be directly beneath the shoulder, at 90° to the floor, and the lifted arm should be extended upwards. An easier alternative is to balance on the elbow rather than the hand to begin with.

figure 3.7 the star position

- Start by lying on the floor on your right hip and right leg, leaning on your right hand.
- Lift the right hip off the floor so that a straight line is made along the long axis of the body, ensuring that the hand is directly underneath the shoulder.
- The natural inclination is for the hips to fall back. It is essential to push the hips forward to hold the straight line and ensure core stability.
- The upper (left) leg may then be lifted (this may not be possible when you first start this exercise) and the left arm should also be lifted so that the left hand points directly upwards (straight line running through right arm, chest and left arm).

Again, remember to keep the core abdominal muscles tight and keep breathing.

Throughout the year your triathlon training will change – this is called periodization. However, it would be a good idea to include some core conditioning training into every week, if not every training session.

Periodization and training periods

Training is a complex issue of building blocks of hard work built upon each other, and it is necessary for early training to be correct so that the blocks added later have a solid foundation. Different periods of the year can be used for different aspects of training. A well-thought-out training plan will alter its main theme for each period of the year. This is called periodization. It is also important that every training session is not always hard; there is a need to include easy sessions as well. Triathlon competition and the racing season in Great Britain and most of Western Europe starts in May and goes through until September. Athletes intending to race would have a logical division of the year similar to that shown below

Off-season/winter/early preparation

September/October to February/March
20–8 weeks

- This period is where the hard background work is done.
- The focus is on endurance (aerobic) exercise and longer

repetitions with short recovery time.

- Strength work can be done on hills in cycling and running.
- Strength work working with paddles in swimming may be done.
- Any weaknesses in technique should also be attended to and rectified.

Pre-season

February/March to April/May
8–16 weeks

- The endurance work and longer repetitions are maintained particularly through the early part of this phase of training.
- Strength work is also maintained.
- More quality is introduced in the guise of faster interval (anaerobic) and repetition training with longer recovery periods.
- Some power training may be started.
- A little more focus on mental attitude (preparing for a race and everything that surrounds it (nervousness, panic, unfounded fears) is also relevant for this phase.

Competitive/racing season

May/June to August/September
14–18 weeks

It is very easy to lose hard-won fitness during the racing season as you focus on races.

- Maintain endurance work if you want to race well through the competitive period and not fall away in performance as the season progresses.
- You must maintain your aerobic fitness while also working on quality to ensure the best performances during races.
- Consider the amount of races you are competing in and adapt the amount of training you do to take account of this.

After/post season

October to November
2–6 weeks

- This is a time of active rest (exercising in different ways at a lower intensity) and recovery.
- Make time to deal with issues with technique that became apparent during the race season.
- Concentrate on mental attitude if necessary.

It is important to note that all these periods of training are not fixed, separate and mutually exclusive from each other. A good, well-thought-out training programme will have elements of several different types of training in each period of the year. The athlete must train to their weaknesses; if there is a lack of speed that means working on this, poor swimming technique means more training in this area. The different training periods will blend into each other gradually, rather than changing suddenly when a new period begins. Complete changes in emphasis can often lead to injury.

With the general principles of training outlined it is time to look in detail at how to train for each discipline of triathlon:

- swimming
- cycling
- running
- transition.

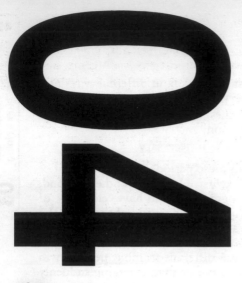

04

swimming

In this chapter you will learn:
- key areas for improvement in swimming
- technique drills
- front crawl full stroke
- how to structure swimming training sessions.

Unless you are lucky enough to have a good swimming background, swimming can be a big worry when you're entering the sport of triathlon. Everyone has run, either as a sport in its own right or as part of almost any team game, and all children learn to ride a bike. However, swimming is different, and although all primary-age schoolchildren have swimming lessons at school and most will learn to swim, it often remains at that level – being able to swim but not necessarily having the confidence to swim in deep water or for any long distance.

Without a swimming background, new triathletes will be at a disadvantage, and need to work on their swimming technique to become both proficient and confident. It is sometimes said that a triathlon is won or lost in the water, where proficient swimmers can gain minutes over those with less technique and speed.

In this chapter you will learn the basic techniques required for front crawl, the main stroke used in triathlon. The drills in this chapter will enable you to improve your swimming and fine-tune your technique, taking valuable seconds, possibly even minutes, off your swim time. You will learn how to do timed swims in training, practise how and when to breathe, and understand the importance of body positioning in the water.

Swimming is often the weakest discipline of many new triathletes, but with a number of valuable insider tips to further decrease your swim time, this chapter might just make this discipline your best.

Differences between pool and open water swimming

The swim section in a triathlon is either in an indoor or outdoor pool, or may be an open water swim in a lake, canal, river or the sea. The specific challenges of open water swimming are discussed in the next chapter – the main differences between an open water and pool swim are:

- You will probably be started in timed sections in a pool swim, whereas an open water start may start all swimmers simultaneously.
- You are more likely to start from within the water in the pool; an open water swim may involve jumping or diving in.

- Visibility is likely to be better in a pool swim, with the advantages of pool lanes and lines helping you to swim in a straight line.
- Swimming in a pool offers the security of being able to either put your feet down, or at least hold on to the side or a lane rope; an open water swim usually has none of these options.

Pool swimming

However, pool swim triathlons can be challenging, with possibly crowded lanes and the likelihood of different standards of swimming ability. Swimmers are normally started at five- or ten-second intervals, and in a 25-metre pool it is easy to see that with perhaps six or more swimmers in each lane that there won't be too much spare room. Another way of starting pool-based swims is to have the swimmers in the pool together holding on to the side at the shallow end of the pool, and when the gun goes for the start, everyone pushes off together. As you can imagine, controlled bedlam can ensue!

Technique, technique, technique!

With many new triathletes coming from running and cycling, it can be daunting and frustrating to understand that the essence of making improvements in swimming comes from endlessly working on technique, rather than more and more hours of physical (and frustrating) effort in the pool. Certainly, hard work in training will make you faster, but only if your technique and your swimming stroke is good. If you go straight into the hard work ethic without taking the time to work on an efficient technique first, you may well find that you will become slower, as that extra effort will actually be a force working against you.

The essence of being a good swimmer – particularly in triathlon where the distance is usually between 400 and 1500 metres – is in possessing a good stroke, and that only comes from working on technique and stroke drills designed to ensure that your swimming is efficient. Attention to technique, particularly in the early stages, will improve your swim stroke beyond recognition. Even excellent swimmers will always do some work on their stroke and technique in every swimming training session.

Which type of swim stroke?

Front crawl (freestyle) is normally the stroke of choice, but there is no restriction on the swimming stroke you must use during a triathlon event, and for beginners, breaststroke and backstroke are perfectly acceptable. However, front crawl is the fastest and most economical stroke when swam properly.

Getting swimming lessons

Joining a swimming club or a triathlon club with a good swimming section is essential. When we run or cycle we can see ourselves and therefore get immediate feedback of what we look like and how we're progressing. In the swimming pool we can't see what we're doing. Swimmers say that a swimming coach is the swimmer's eyes on the poolside, and this is absolutely true. You must have a swimming coach or swimming teacher to help you progress.

Top tip

Even though swimming is the shortest part of the race, technique (while also important in cycling and running) is absolutely essential, and learning correct technique will ensure that you can finish the swim discipline in good time.

Many swimming clubs now have 'masters' sections that cater for adult swimmers, and local authorities often have adult learner groups. These may be early morning, during quiet periods during the day or in the (usually late) evening. Points of contact to find swimming lessons or swimming coaches near you are:

- **www.britishtriathlon.org**
- the amateur swimming association, **www.britishswimming.org**
- your local authority
- try the local swimming pool for adult learner sessions.

Areas for improvement in swimming

Swimming teachers and coaches talk about **BLABT** when introducing novice swimmers to improvers' classes. BLABT stands for:

Body
Legs
Arms
Breathing
Timing

Body

- The swimmer should aim to be flat, horizontal, stretched and streamlined when swimming front crawl.
- A good head position coupled with a balancing leg kick are the two essentials to a flat, streamlined body position.
- Keeping the head in line with the body, with eyes looking forward and down (around 45°) will maintain a flat body; lifting the head or looking backwards will take the body away from the streamlined position.
- The head should remain looking down apart from when breathing, and the shoulders and upper body should rotate to the chin rather than the other way round.

Legs

A good leg kick is absolutely essential for an effective front crawl. However, the emphasis must be on using the legs for balance rather than propulsion. Over-kicking and working the legs too hard will be counter-productive as the large leg muscles will use a lot of oxygen that is better used by the upper body.

- The leg kick starts from the hips rather than the knees; kicking from the knees will unbalance both the stroke and the body position, and will create drag that will slow down your swimming speed.
- The kick should be shallow rather than deep and within the body zone, although it must be deep enough to work effectively.
- The ankles need to be both loose and flexible at all times. The more flexible the ankles, the more effective the kick.

The equalizer

For open water training and competition, remember that wearing a wetsuit adds a great deal of buoyancy (a huge advantage to the nervous or poor swimmer, so much so that elite triathletes call the wetsuit the 'equalizer') so that anything other than a very light kick to balance the stroke will be wasted.

To summarize:

- Kick continuously.
- Kick with legs long, with flexible knees and ankles.
- Kick within the body depth.
- Kick from the hips.

Arms

The arm and body action can be split into two phases:

- the initial pull
- the push away.

Let's take a look at technique for the initial pull.

Initial pull

Although the arms are the main propulsion for swimming, the big muscles in the back (latissimus dorsi, called 'lats') and chest (pectoral muscles, called 'pecs') are vital for ensuring speed and power. The upper arm muscles (biceps and triceps) are much smaller and will fatigue far more quickly. It is essential that upper body rotation is learnt so that these big back and chest muscles can be used efficiently.

- The hand should enter the water between the shoulder and the centre line of the body (middle of the head).
- The hand enters the water approximately 30–60 cm in front of the head and slides forward in a streamlined action just below the surface for another 20–25 cm.
- While the arm is sliding forward, the body is rotating, which ensures maximum reach.
- The fingertips should be the lowest point as the arm reaches full extension.
- The wrist is flexed and the elbow tensed.

- It is important that the elbow does not drop lower than the wrist at any time during the propulsive or recovery phase of the front crawl stroke.
- The elbow remains higher than the wrist; the wrist remains higher than the fingers.
- The hand presses briefly downwards and then backwards. Rather than pulling backwards, what we are really trying to do is to 'fix' the arm and hand and pull the body over this fixed position.

The push away
As the body is pulled forward over the arm and the initial pull changes to a push away, the hand will be directly under the body with a slight bend at the elbow. From this position the push backwards starts the second, back part of the stroke.

- The hand exits the water with the thumb down when the thumb is alongside the thigh. Poorer swimmers will allow the hand to leave the water too quickly and lose valuable speed and length of stroke.
- A good recovery is reliant on both shoulder mobility and rotation with the elbow once again being the highest part of the arm as it travels forward smoothly and close to the

swimmer's body. Recovering too wide (little rotation, poor shoulder flexibility) will take the body away from the desired flat, streamlined position.

- The arm should be as relaxed as possible during the recovery phase.

The entire arm stroke is a gradual acceleration with an initial fix on the water for entry and catch, and the greatest speed on the second (push) part of the stroke.

Swimmers and swimming coaches often talk about the 'S pull'. This refers to the shallow figure 'S' that the hand makes as it progresses through the propulsive phase. I believe that the teaching of the 'S' pull is often overemphasized and will develop naturally.

Coordination of breathing and timing

The coordination of breathing and timing is often seen as one of the most difficult aspects of swimming front crawl. As the leading hand and arm passes underneath the chest, the other arm (the recovering arm) enters the water to begin the propulsive phase. Many new swimmers think that the propulsive phase for one arm begins as the other arm is just starting the recovery phase. If this were true, the whole swimming action would be continuously slowing and accelerating, thus slowing down the swimmer's speed considerably.

Timing for breathing should fit in with the timing for the arm action.

- When breathing to the right, as your right hand enters the water, begin to breathe out.
- Your face is submerged and you breathe out under the water.
- As the right hand reaches the end of propulsive phase and is just about to start the recovery, allow your head to turn to the right in line with your body as it rotates, and breathe in.

For breathing to the left, just substitute left for right.

It cannot be emphasized enough how important it is to turn the head in line with the body rather than lifting the head as a separate action. A poor breathing technique and action is one of the most common faults in taking the body away from its streamlined position.

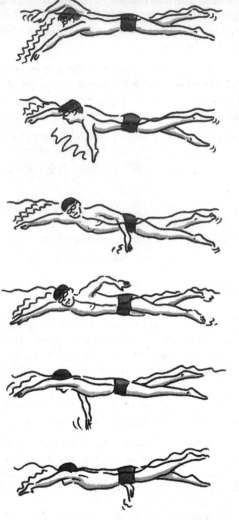

a) the right arm starts to enter the water, the left arm starts the pull

b) the right arm has now completely entered the water, the left arm changes from pulling to pushing the water

c) the swimmer breathes to the left as the left arm and hand push back hard

d) the left arm begins the recovery phase and the swimmer returns to the face-down position; the body rotates to its maximum on the left side

e) the left arm has now completely entered the water, the right arm changes from pulling to pushing the water

f) the right arm and hand push back hard but the swimmer doesn't need to breathe on this side

g) the right arm begins the recovery phase; the left arm starts the pull; the body rotates to its maximum on the right side

figure 4.1 one full front crawl stroke

Poor breathing timing is often caused by 'windmilling' – rushing the stroke, making it too fast and inefficient. Simply slowing the stroke down, even as much as a 'catch-up' stroke (see drills section in this chapter), will go a long way to smoothing out the coordination, breathing and timing.

> **Improving your front crawl swimming**
>
> There are three areas that are essential to improving your front crawl, particularly important for open water swimming.
>
> 1 Identifying drag (streamlining) and implementing a correct kick.
> 2 Introduce rotation.
> 3 Learning the extended position – a vital position to progress onto further drills.
>
> These three skills are completely inter-related and depend on each other. A strong leg kick for balance will maintain a flat, streamlined body position and will make it easier to implement rotation.

Swimming drills

There are many drills in swimming that contribute to an excellent technique. However, it is important that the drills are used specifically to improve each aspect of the front crawl stroke and not merely used because they are there. There are a progressive series of front crawl drills that will assist the athlete in reaching an excellent technique.

The four key concepts that are required to help the athlete swim faster, smoother and more efficiently through the water are:

1 **Lengthen the pull** – The more distance travelled per stroke means fewer strokes per length and fewer strokes needed to complete the distance you need to swim in competitions. You must catch the stroke properly in the first instance to start a more powerful pull phase.
2 **Start to swim on your side** (rotation principle) – This will minimize your frontal resistance, bringing into play the stronger muscles of your back for a more powerful pull whilst automatically lengthening your stroke.
3 **The timing of the stroke** – Work away from the arms performing at opposites (windmilling) and develop a three-quarter catch-up or near catch-up front crawl full stroke.

4 **Stop relying on your legs** – The legs are not very good at keeping you afloat or propelling you forward so try to not use them for this purpose.

figure 4.2 rotation of the body seen from two angles

Flotation

Even the least able floaters in the water can improve by stretching out and making themselves as long and streamlined as possible. A windmill style of stroke keeps a lot of the upper body's weight centred around the head. This style of front crawl reduces the overall length of the body, while a near catch-up style of front crawl leaves the lead arm outstretched and lengthens body length.

Streamlining

Drills working on streamlining help to overcome frontal water resistance. The athlete should focus on a central head position in line with the body (eyes looking forward but face not facing forwards), toes pointed, legs straight, arms outstretched and tight to the head. Arms spread apart ('starfish position') will immediately reduce forward momentum. Compared to the starfish position, you will travel twice as far in the streamlined position for the same amount of energy.

These progressive drills and practices will work towards these important key concepts. Many of the drills below are already known, however, there may be different terminology for some of them.

Body position kicking drill
Start practising this on your back as it takes away the difficulty of breathing for the new triathlete. As with all new drills when first introduced, it is helpful to wear fins to keep the body horizontal in the water. When you are ready, try the drill on your front and remove the fins.

- Ensure good alignment from head to toes.
- Raise the head every six kicks to breathe.
- Head position on front should be comfortable with eyes looking forward but not facing forwards.
- Keep eyes looking down and forward towards the bottom of the pool.
- Keep hips high, stomach just breaking the surface.
- Ensure the kick is from the hip (not the knees), and in an upward and downward plane.
- Keep ankles loose, toes plantarflexed (pointed) however, avoid floppy ankles.
- Avoid locking the toes so they are pointing downwards to the bottom of the pool — turn the toes slightly inwards towards each other.
- Kick the legs in a shallow plane, just a few inches in depth, and feel the big toes brushing together.

Torpedo drill
- Start on your back then try on your front. Start with the same body position as for body position kicking drill.
- Leg kicking as above, hips relaxed but stable. Try to initiate the rotation from the upper body.
- Hips should never get more than two inches below the surface.
- The shoulders and hips should be rolling from side to side, pausing as the shoulder gets to the lowest point under the water.
- The shoulder turns to the chin rather than the chin turning to the shoulder. Rotate as far as comfortable but do not over exert by moving the chin down to the shoulder.

- Feet and ankles stay loose; kick will shift slightly from side to side as the body rolls.
- Breathing needs to be timed to fit in with the body rotation.
- Keep your head still.

When performing torpedo drills on your back, imagine that you are dropping your lower shoulder rather then lifting your upper shoulder to your chin. It may help you feel smoother.

Extension of the torpedo drills

1. Basic extension

- Body should be rolled on side, one arm extended from the shoulder, reaching in front of the body.
- Very little space should be present between head and extending arm.
- Try to have a straight line extending from the tips of fingers through to the toes.
- Hold this body position on one side for between three and five seconds, then switch arms underwater while body rotates to opposite side with the other arm now leading in front.
- Maintain the steady relaxed kicking from body position kicking and torpedo drills.
- Breathe every six kicks, then roll into one full stroke to take you onto your other side.

Top tips

Remember:

- shoulder to chin rotation
- legs kicking in vertical plane
- aim to have the trail shoulder above the surface of the water.

---

2. Shark fin up/down

- Begin the drill in the same position as above, arm extended, perfect alignment on side from fingers to toes.
- The trailing arm should begin to rise out of the water, bending at the elbow to bring hand to head.
- The high, bent elbow creates a 'shark fin' position above the head as the hand stays loose under a high-arched elbow.
- After a two-second pause, the arm returns to position on side, pausing for two more seconds.

- The arm then completes full recovery going forward towards the extension position, following the same path as before (high elbow, loose hand, shark fin).
- Once the hands have come together, stretched one above the other, the body rotates while the next arm pulls through to the hip.
- Pause in the extended position (now on opposite side). Begin drill again with new arm.

Catch-up drill

- One arm and hand are extended in front of the head.
- The hand remains there until the other hand reaches forward to touch the first hand, and the first hand then starts the pull phase.
- At the start of this pull, the body is flat with the chest pointing downwards rather than rotating. You may feel that this flat start position with the arms outstretched is not particularly well streamlined, but as the pull starts and the body rolls up onto the side, the streamlining and position should feel better.

Variations of catch-up

1. Head/shoulder tap

- The hands must touch at the beginning of each stroke in the extended position. Focus on one arm at a time aiming at full rotation from side to side.
- The hands recover as the body rotates to one side, with a high elbow keeping the hands low and relaxed.
- As the fingers pass the shoulder, they should physically touch the shoulder or the head to keep the body rotated, and to ensure the high elbow remains.
- After the head or shoulder tap, the hand moves towards the entry position as the body begins its rotation onto the other side.
- The hands connect in the extension position and the opposite hand begins the drill.

2. Elbow pause

In this drill, continue to focus on the 'catch-up' timing with good body rotation and a high elbow recovery.

- The hand passes the shoulder and head, the fingers then pause as the fingertips almost touch the surface of the water.

- The fingertips should be next to and opposite the elbow of the currently extended arm. Hold this position for two seconds, and then the hand continues into the water as the body rotates.
- Keep the hand from entering too near to the head or too far away from the head.
- The opposite arm pulls through under the water and follows the same pattern.
- Pause the recovering hand in line with the outstretched elbow of the lead arm. Usually the hand is paused above the surface of the water, but for an extra cue as to where the hands should be entering, allow the fingers to slide under the water a few inches and pause in line with the submerged elbow.
- Once the two-second pause has elapsed, rotate the body around in time with the paused hand gliding forwards while the already outstretched hand then starts the catch.

Catch drills

Short doggy paddle (puppy paddle)

The body should be held in the streamline position. With this drill it is worth using fins or a pull buoy to support body weight and help balance.

- The arms should be extended forward in front of the head.
- Bending at the elbow, the hand and forearm act as a single paddle and push water backwards.
- As the hand and forearm reach a 90°-degree bend, the hand returns to the start position and the other arm then performs the same exercise.
- There should be little to no movement in the shoulder and upper arm and the wrist should be held rigid.
- The hands should push back in line just outside the shoulders.

Doggy paddle

The body should be held in the streamline position. As with the previous drill it is worth using fins or a pull buoy to support body weight and help balance.

- The arms should be extended forward in front of the head.
- Bending at the elbow, the hand and forearm act as a paddle and push water backwards.

- At the 90°-degree bend, the body begins to rotate onto the left side as the right arm continues pushing water back all the way towards the hips.
- The hand should finish at the hip as the body is completely rotated onto the left side.
- There is a brief pause before the arm slides underwater and returns to the front.

Essentially, this is a front crawl stroke with the recovery underneath the water. However, from a rotation point of view, when the hands are 'caught up' in front, the body is flat, and when starting the catch you should feel the rotation start and your body slip sideways.

Top tips

- Keep the head still at all times.
- The hands and elbows stay below the water at all times.
- The wrist must be rigid when starting the catch.
- The hand should accelerate right through the propulsive phase.
- The hands recover under the water, close to the body with the palms facing upwards.

Doggy paddle switch

The body should be held in the streamline position. Again, it is worth using fins or a pull buoy to support body weight and help balance.

- The arms should be extended forward in front of the head.
- Bending at the elbow, the hand and forearm act as a paddle and push water backwards.
- At the 90°-degree bend, the body begins to rotate onto the left side as the right arm continues pushing water back all the way towards the hips.
- The hand should finish at the hip as the body is completely rotated onto the left side.
- As the arm recovers under the water, the opposite hand begins the process.

This switch drill is the same as the doggy paddle drills, except that the arms are simultaneously pulling and recovering. The rotation of the body is the key element here, the rotation sets the timing and helps drive the paddle through the water.

Single arm drill

- In a flat, head-down position, with both arms stretched forwards and using a gentle kick (wear fins if needed), execute a strong catch and accelerate one hand under the body, down and through to the hips, before exiting and recovering back to the other hand still placed stretched out in front of the body.
- The **same** arm and hand then repeat the action.
- Feel the catch and surge forwards, helping you to rotate up onto your side.

If this catch and acceleration is done well it is possible to feel the difference between the flat, initial, non-streamlined position compared to the rotated, on-the-side, streamlined position during the stroke.

Variations of single arm drill

1. Single arm submerged switch (SASS)

This drill is similar to the doggy paddle drill, however, each phase of the drill finishes with both arms at the sides of the body.

- Start in the extension position with one arm stretched out and one arm held by the side.
- Take a breath, and then execute a catch with the outstretched arm while rotating.
- Finish with both arms down at your sides, with the body on the opposite side.
- Finally, recover the lower arm back out in front, taking you back to the extended position on the opposite side.
- Keep the hand flat on the submerged recovery to avoid pressure on the shoulders.

2. Advanced single arm drill

The non-pulling arm trails at the side of the body. The head remains perfectly still other than when breathing. Combine rotation of the upper body with the following points:

- forward extension of the arm (pierce the water with fingers first and wrist rigid, followed by the elbow, the hand should glide forwards parallel to the surface of the water)
- the catch phase
- the main pull of the body over the hand
- the final acceleration phase of the hand.

You should feel the acceleration of the body over the hand at the back of the stroke as the final push with the triceps muscle drives the body forward. Pause momentarily as the hand gets to its fullest extension in front, then take a breath to the side of the unused arm. Once the head is back to the neutral position, start the next catch.

Full stroke practice

Drills are only a means to an end. It is essential that full stroke front crawl is practised as well in between the drills. Follow these top ten tips to put all the aspects of front crawl together.

1 A still head, looking down and slightly forward.
2 Legs staying long and relaxed.
3 Small kicks generated by the upper leg not the knees, toes pointing towards the back of pool.
4 Body rotation equal on both sides.
5 Arms extending and pausing at the front of the stroke, not rushing into the pulling phase until the recovering arm has passed the head.
6 The initial movement in the pulling arm coming from bending the elbow to create a strong, stable paddle.
7 Once the catch and paddle has been created, the rotation of the body begins to help drive the hand through the water to create forward movement.
8 The propulsive movement of the hand finishes at the hips with the arm almost straight, rather than finishing early at waist level with the arm still very bent at the elbow.
9 The recovering arm stays relaxed, bending at the elbow and with the elbow held high.
10 As each hand enters the water, ensure the fingertips enter first, with the arm extended forwards and away from the head so as not to let the hand drive downwards immediately.

Top tip

Every hand and arm movement is from slow to fast, and the learning process should reflect that. The new swimmer and triathlete must be able to swim drills, execute technique work and full stroke efficiently at a slow speed before gradually increasing the pace. At a faster speed a good, efficient stroke technique should be maintained.

Feeling the water

The feel of the water is critical to improvement. It is important that the swimmer learns to feel the water. This is far more important in the early stages than attempting to swim fast. Switching between an exaggerated poor technique and an excellent technique highlights the difference and makes the swimmer aware when good technique is being used. Implementing the technique points in this chapter and then reversing them before going back to a good technique will focus attention on the differences. Key points for success are as follows:

1 The fingers start the pull first in front crawl, so it is essential that a firm, fixed wrist position is maintained when pulling.
2 Frontal resistance is huge when swimming. A flat body position along the long axis is essential.
3 Rotation is essential. The hips initiate this immediately before the hands start the pull.

Swimming training

Initially, new triathletes will want to get used to swimming distance, and to swimming it on front crawl stroke. However, once the aim of being able to swim continuously (400–800 metres) and comfortably is achieved, then it is time to look for proper, controlled swimming sessions. Often it can be difficult for an adult novice swimmer to join a swimming club. The majority of swimming clubs are aimed at teenagers and younger age groups, and are competitive. Some swimming clubs do have a 'masters' group where adult swimmers, often triathletes, do have appropriate coached swimming sessions. In addition to this, many triathlon clubs will have coached swimming sessions for adults.

If this is not available, triathletes should seek advice and try to liaise and arrange to meet with other triathletes, and swim in public pool sessions. In order to try to work out a training schedule, triathletes must be aware that the swimming discipline of a triathlon is distance-orientated (400, 750 or 1500 metres), and the content of the training session should reflect this. As a rule of thumb, a swimming session should contain all or most of the following:

- **the warm-up** – between 10 and 25 per cent of the training session
- **the subset** – to raise heart rate and get the body ready to exercise
- **the first cool-down** – this can be optional and often includes drills and technique
- **the main set** – the hard work element, between 30 and 50 per cent of the training session
- **the second cool-down** – again, usually with a technique or stroke content
- **the warm-down or swim down** – slower swimming, a reflection on the session and a chance for the body to relax.

Frequently, the first or second cool-down will be omitted. It is essential that at an early stage of swimming training technique is emphasized at all times. As much as two-thirds of the training session can be aerobic, and as little as one-quarter of the session performed at anaerobic or speed level. There is little need for maximum speed in triathlon swimming training. Newcomers to swimming sometimes comment that swimming training can be boring. If you are attending a coached session, then it is up to the coach to make the session interesting, appropriate and challenging. If you are coaching yourself, then it becomes your responsibility. Swimming technique will improve more quickly if you work on short repetitions and take adequate recovery in between the repetitions.

Swimming programmes

A number of linked and progressive swimming sessions are set out in Chapter 11. In addition, set out below are a number of detailed swimming training sessions that triathletes can use and alter to their own needs. These training sessions assume a swimming pool of 25 metres in length, and contain the technique and swimming drills already discussed. All of the sessions are suitable for training periods throughout the year, however, the first four sessions are progressive, and focused very much on technique, being particularly suitable during the off-season build-up. Sessions 5–8 focus less on technique and more on pace, but also include some technique work.

Swimming training session 1

Remember to follow all the technique points already discussed regarding arm, head and body positioning, kick depth and rotation. The first part of the session practises kicking and upper body movements without the arms interfering.

Kicking

Warm-up	200-metre swim.
Introducing a correct leg kick	8 × 25 metres kicking (four lengths on your back, four on front*). Arms outstretched or with a float.
Repeat in the deep end	Vertical kicking – 4 × 20 seconds kicking. 20 seconds rest (hang on the side of the pool).
100-metre swim	Use a smaller, less 'dragging' kick from the hip, legs straight with knees not locked.
Kick practice introducing upper body rotation	Practise first in the shallow end standing upright. This can be included in warm-up i.e. swim two lengths (2 × 25 metres) then practise ten standing rotations. Repeat seven times (400-metre swim completed).
Torpedo drill on back with fins	4–8 × 25 metres.
Repeat torpedo drill on front	4–8 × 25 metres with 20 seconds rest at the end of each 25-metre length. Hold breath for as long as possible then break into full stroke to complete the length; aim for a half-length of the drill.

100-metre swim	Feel a smaller, shallower less 'dragging' kick. Feel the movement of the upper body practised in the last drill taking shape in the full stroke swim.

*Alternate with and without fins. If you cannot use fins then attempt a half-length kicking before completing the length with full stroke front crawl.

Now we will introduce the arm movements. If the body is rotating well you should find it easier to recover the arms.

Arm recovery

Single arm free	8 × 25 metres.
	Push off with both arms outstretched in front.
	A pull buoy can aid with balance by holding it outstretched with the arm not pulling.
	Every two seconds/six kicks do a full single arm pull.
	Change arms each length.
Extension drill with fins	8 × 25 metres.
	Breathe every six kicks in the 'superman' position.
	Use fins and pull buoy as balance for the outstretched arm.
	The float should be submerged in line with the depth of the shoulder*.
Extension switch drill	8 × 25 metres.
	Breathe every six kicks while holding the 'superman' position then roll into three full strokes between kicks.
	Aim to have the trail shoulder above the surface of the water.

| Rotation reminder – Torpedo alternate lengths on front/back | 4 × 50 metres. |
| Swim cool-down | 200 metres. |

*The float assists with balance and gives the lead arm support since without fins some might struggle.

Swimming training session 2

Warm-up	200-metre swim without fins.
Full stroke front crawl	8 × 25 metres with ten seconds rest after each length.
	Concentrate on one aspect of the stroke on each length:
	• keep the head still when not breathing • shallow leg kick • feel the big toes brushing against each other • upper body rotation • early catch • push through to the back of the stroke.
Rotation practice	4–6 × 75 metres.
Torpedo drill	3 × 25 metres on your back.
	25 metres on front (break into full stroke free when running low on air).
	25 metres on your front with a breath on each third rotation
	Aim for six kicks during each rotation.
	Rest for 30 seconds after each 75 metres.

100-metre swim	Use a smaller, less 'dragging' kick.
	Feel the movement of the upper body rotation drills taking shape in the full stroke swim.
Kick and rotation	4×25 metres.
Extension drill	Breathe every six kicks.
	Use fins and a pull buoy as balance for the outstretched arm.
	Float should be submerged in line with depth of the shoulder.
Extension switch drill with fins	8×25 metres. Perform six kicks in fully extended position, breathe, then roll into three strokes between every six kicks.
	Try to breathe during the kick rather than the full stroke sections.
100-metre swim	Use a smaller, less 'dragging' kick.
	Feel the movement of the upper body rotation drills taking shape in the full stroke swim.
Full strokes basics	4×25 metres full stroke front crawl.
Finger trail drill	Fingertips only to be dragging through the water and increase upper body rotation to help keep the elbows high.
100-metre swim	Breathe bilaterally.
	Count the number of strokes per length and attempt to 'subtract a stroke' each 25-metre length.
	Increase the range of upper body rotation and really stretch out into the stroke.

Advanced rotation practice	4×50 metres.
Doggy paddle	Catch-up style on every other length by swimming back full stroke on the even lengths, fully extending into a side-on, streamlined position at the finish of stroke.
	25 metres on front (break into full stroke free when running low on air).
	25 metres on your front with a breath on each third rotation.
	Aim for six kicks during each rotation.
	Rest 30 seconds after each 75 metres.
Push and glide reminder	2×25 metres.
	First length glue upper arms to ears, point toes.
	Second length starfish position.
	Note how you travel twice as far in the streamlined position.
100-metre swim	Use a smaller, less 'dragging' kick.
	Feel the movement of the upper body rotation drills taking shape in the full stroke swim.
Timing introduction	8×25 metres.
Catch-up drill	Mix alternate lengths near catch-up with full catch-up (leading hand out in front until the other hand catches up).
	Eventually the full stroke should become a mix of the two styles.

| Full stroke swimming to finish | 12 × 25 metre swims, six with fins, six without fins. |
| | Breathing pattern – one length right, one length left, one length bilateral. |

Swimming training session 3

Warm-up	200-metre swim without fins.
Kick reminder	8 × 25 metres, four with fins, four without.
	Swim this as push and glide then 15 kicks underwater in the streamlined position before the first swimming stroke*.
More rotation practice	8 × 25 metres.
Extension drill	Fins optional – as improvements start try to use them less frequently.
	Ten kicks on the left, one stroke, ten kicks on the right then complete rest of length full stroke with shoulder to chin rotation.
50-metre swim	Use a smaller, less 'dragging' kick.
	Feel the movement of the upper body rotation drills taking shape in the full stroke swim.
Torpedo kick	8 × 25 metres.
	Alternate 25 metres on your front and back. Aim for halfway on the 'front torpedoes' before breaking into full stroke to complete the length.

50-metre swim	Feel the movement of the upper body rotation drills taking shape in the full stroke swim.
Extension drill	4 × 25 metres. Breathe every six kicks. No fins but use a pull buoy for balance for the outstretched arm. Float should be submerged in line with depth of the shoulder.
Rotation with arm recovery **Shark fin drill**	8 × 25 metres. 25 metre left arm sharking, 25 metre right arm sharking. Start with the basic extension position. Swim four lengths with a breath taken between shark fin recoveries, and four lengths watching the arm recover.
100-metre swim	Feel the movement of the upper body rotation drills taking shape in the full stroke swim.
Timing **Half length water polo drill (see Chapter 05) into half length swim**	8 × 25 metres. Focus on the hand entering in line with the elbow of the outstretched arm. Aim for the entering hand to cause no bubbles on entry. Accelerate through the stroke – hand movement is slow to fast. Do not start the 'catch' of the outstretched arm until the recovering arm has nearly caught up.

Elbow pause with submerged fingers and fins	8 × 25 metres. Pause the recovering hand in line with the outstretched elbow of the lead arm.
	Usually we pause the hand above the surface of the water: allow the fingers to slide under the water a few inches and pause in line with the submerged elbow. Once the paused duration has elapsed, rotate the body through in time with the paused hand gliding forwards while the already outstretched hand then starts the catch.
50-metre swim	Feel a smaller, shallower less 'dragging' kick. Feel the timing change to the stroke taking shape in the full stroke swim.
Doggy paddle (full switch style) Catch-up with fins	4 × 75 metres (25 metres doggy paddle, 25 metres catch-up and 25 metres catch-up with fins).
200-metre swim	Feel the timing change to the stroke taking shape in the full stroke swim.

*Streamline tightly off the wall, don't rush into the kick, and use the speed off of the wall.

Swimming training session 4

Warm-up	200-metre swim without fins.
Rotation	4×25 metres.
Torpedo drill	Swim on your front with a breath each third rotation – breath and body rotation are two separate movements.
50-metre swim	Feel a smaller, shallower less 'dragging' kick. Feel the timing change to the stroke taking shape in the full stroke swim.
Extension drill	4×25 metres.
Fins optional	Breathe every six kicks.
	Use a pull buoy to balance outstretched arm.
	Aim for a fully rotated position so that the shoulder rotates around to the chin.
Rotation with arm recovery	8×25 metres.
	25 metres left arm sharking, 25 metres right arm sharking.
	Elbows pointing to the ceiling on recovery.
	Swim four lengths with breath taken between shark fin recoveries and four watching the arm recover.
100-metre swim	Feel a smaller, shallower less 'dragging' kick. Feel the timing change to the stroke taking shape in the full stroke swim.
Catch	4×50-metre full stroke front crawl, relaxed swimming – think about how your normal catch looks/feels like.

| Catch (continued) | Try a few strokes with a perfectly straight arm and feel how uncomfortable this is.

Turn the head enough to get a quick breath, no higher then the gutters of the pool. |
|---|---|
| **Sculling** is a drill that is used to get your hands used to the change in position through the stroke. The palms of the hands face outwards and the hands and arms push sideways; as the hands pass the shoulder line, the pitch of the hands change to inwards, again as they almost come together below the chest, the pitch changes to outwards again. Basically it is a 'push out sideways, and pull in together' movement.

Hand positions for correct pull to catch | 3 × 50 metres.

50 metres with arms out straight in front, mild change in pitch of the hands rolling back and forth.

50 metres with arms in a mid-point position, hands 30 centimetres below the surface of the water, elbows bent at 90°.

50 metres with hands inside the elbows, fingertips pointing to the bottom of the pool. Elbows wide of the body and bent at 90°. |
| **100 metres fast swimming** | Feel a better 'grip' on the water using the scull into catch position through the hands pathway under the body. |
| **Puppy paddle with half pull** | 4 × 25 metres with fins.

Focus on catch.

Push off with both hands outstretched.

Kick to the surface.

Perform a small scull into catch keeping the pathway of the hand central, the elbow high and wide. |

100 metres fast swimming	No fins. Feel a better 'grip' on the water using the scull into catch position through the hands pathway under the body.
Extension to catch	8 × 25 metres (alternate 25 metres to the left, 25 metres to the right).
	Perform a small catch with fins every 6–8 kicks.
	Push off from the wall into a streamlined 'superman' position; focus on good upper body rotation with a small flutter kick.
	One arm outstretched, lower shoulder rotated fully so it is next to the chin.
200-metre swim	Feel all the drills taking shape within the full stroke.

Swimming training session 5

Warm-up	400 metres as repetitions of 50 metres front crawl, 25 metres length of choice.
	20 seconds recovery.
	200 metres kicking with fins, 50 metres of choice and 25 metres front crawl.
	20 seconds recovery.
	200 metres drill as repetitions of 50 metres front crawl and 25 metres choice stroke drill.
Main set	6 × 200 metres with second and fifth 200 metres as emphasis on stroke technique and one aspect of drill.

| Stroke technique work | 3 × 50 metres catch-up (hold the hand and arm position in place for a count of three seconds), then 4 × 25 metres full stroke. |
| Warm-down | Easy 200 metres of your choice. |

Swimming training session 6 – Focus on race pace

Warm-up	200 metres stroke of choice.
	6 × 100 metres (2 × 100 metres kicking (fins), 2 × 100 metres drill [repeat three arm strokes then six kicks each side], 2 × 100 metres pulling).
Main set	1 × 200 metres front crawl, rest one minute.
	1 × 150 metres front crawl, rest 45 seconds.
	2 × 100 metres front crawl, rest 30 seconds.
	2 × 50 front crawl, rest 20 seconds.
	Repeat.
Warm-down	75 metres drill (high elbow, arm hesitation).
	25 metres full stroke.
	Repeat × 2.

Swimming training session 7

Warm-up	200 metres stroke of choice.
	200 metres as single arms, up on right arm, back on left arm.
	2 × 100 metres on two drills: fingertip trail and hesitation.
	200 metres choice if time.
Main set	1 × 400 metres front crawl pulling with paddles and pull buoy.
	Rest 45 seconds.
	2 × 200 metres front crawl pulling, pull buoy, no paddles (30 seconds rest between lengths).
	4 × 100 metres front crawl, kicking, fins (15 seconds rest intervals).
	8 × 50 metres front crawl (15 seconds rest intervals).
Warm-down	Alternate 25 metres on backstroke and front crawl for a distance of 400 metres.

Swimming training session 8

Warm-up	100 metres front crawl.
	100 metres backstroke.
	4 × 100 metres kick (fins) as front crawl, backstroke, front crawl, backstroke.
	100 metres backstroke.
	100 metres front crawl.

Main set	All at 400/800 metre race pace.
	1 × 200 metres front crawl pulling with paddles and pull buoy.
	Rest 30 seconds.
	8 × 50 metres front crawl (15 seconds rest intervals).
	Rest 30 seconds.
	2 × 100 metres front crawl pulling with paddles and pull buoy (20 seconds rest intervals and 30 seconds after second 100 metres).
	4 × 25 metres front crawl (20 seconds rest intervals). Rest 30 seconds.
	2 × 100 metres front crawl pulling with paddles and pull buoy (20 seconds rest intervals and 30 seconds after second 100 metres).
	4 × 50 metres front crawl (15 seconds rest intervals).
	Rest 30 seconds.
	1 × 200 metres front crawl pulling with paddles and pull buoy.
Warm-down	200 metres alternating 25 metres front crawl and backstroke.

So, with all these drills and swimming training, your swim stroke should be in good enough shape for you to take to the open water. Read on to learn about all the aspects of open water swimming in a triathlon.

05

open water swimming

In this chapter you will learn:
- what to expect in open water swimming
- how to adapt your start, mid-race and end-of-swim
- drills and techniques
- racing strategies.

If your first triathlon race is going to involve an open water swim, you need to be aware of what is involved, and how to prepare for the essential differences that you will experience between open water and pool swimming. Certain techniques must be learned for open water, but the essentials of a good stroke and a good technique remain constant for both.

Often, newcomers think that swimming in open water is very different to swimming in a warm pool, and that your technique has to change to combat the open water. It is true that the elements of weather, cold, and water conditions will have a big impact on how you swim, but the essential elements of pool and open water swimming are the same: good technique in the pool will equal good technique in open water. The only reasons why good pool swimmers might not swim well outside is when other factors come into play: disorientation, cold, new and/or restricting wetsuits, feelings of claustrophobia in a wetsuit, feelings of agoraphobia in deep water, and other similar issues. Triathletes who have come from an excellent swimming background generally become excellent triathlon swimmers. Good pool swimmers do make good triathlon swimmers so long as appropriate adjustments are made in training and to open water conditions.

This chapter explains what adjustments need to be made when swimming in open water, giving you a good idea of what to expect and how to prepare for your first open water race. By practising the open water drills and skills, and using the tips for open water swimming, you are assured of a thorough and effective preparation for race day.

Open water can feel an alien environment, particularly to weaker swimmers, and there are a number of factors that can contribute to feelings of unease. It's very possible to do most of your swimming training in a swimming pool, but it will be an advantage, and certainly improve your confidence, if you are able to swim in open water before the event. If you do intend to do so, then ensure that you take account of all the usual safety precautions – under no circumstances ever swim alone.

The swim is frequently the most worrying aspect of your first race, particularly if it is your first open water swim. Your imagination plays havoc, and visions of being accidentally kicked or punched, of your goggles becoming dislodged, of becoming breathless and even of being drowned are not uncommon. The thought that you might get into serious trouble and that no one will see you is a more common thought than most people realize. However, some swimmers prefer an open water swim to racing in a pool.

Benefits of an open water swim

Swimming is usually the first discipline in triathlon and this can make it the biggest worry to new triathletes. This worry can easily become panic with the realization that the swim may be in a lake, river, or in the sea. However, some triathletes prefer an open water swim to pool swims as there is a large amount of water to swim in, less crowding, and it is possible to hang back or swim at the edge of the group if you are nervous.

The start

There are a variety of possible starts in open water:

- You can start on the water's edge and run or walk in.
- You may be placed in the water standing on the bottom.
- It is possible that for a deep water start you may be treading water.
- There are occasions when the start is a dive from a pontoon placed in deep water.

In very big events (the London triathlon had over 10000 starters last year!) the start will be split into section categories. These are normally by gender and age bands (usually but not always in five-year bands) so, for example, men aged between 45 and 49 years old will swim against each other, women aged 20 to 24 years old will start together, and so on.

Panic at the start

If the swimming discipline is in open water you will have to deal with the cold, the waves, the wind, and being very close to fellow competitors – being bumped and jostled by them. You often need to wear a wetsuit and lose the 'feel' of the water that you normally have, and may experience feelings of panic or not being able to breathe normally, particularly when you are in the middle of a bunch of swimmers with arms and legs flailing about – open water swimming for the first time can seem like bedlam. There can be literally hundreds of other athletes all fighting for the same water space. There is enormous pressure to avoid trouble during the inevitable rough start, and a feeling that everybody is encroaching on your water space.

If you are a nervous swimmer, you can overcome and avoid this by getting away from other competitors by:

- getting immediately ahead
- placing yourself at the back
- moving to the side at the start and swimming a slightly wider line around.

Getting to the back or to the side are options for the weaker or non-confident swimmers who, by holding back a little on the swim, will lose only minimal time. However, despite this commonsense attitude, the sheer competitiveness of triathletes ensures that almost everybody in your start-wave will be striving for a fast start to ensure that they can stay with the pack of swimmers and take advantage of the legal drafting situation allowed (drafting is covered later in this chapter). This means that the start of the swim is going to be flat-out, leading to oxygen debt, and a feeling of breathlessness and loss of control.

You can try to simulate conditions of an open water start in the pool. Starting four, five or six swimmers together, side-by-side in one lane gives that feeling of tightness and closeness. This number can be increased so that swimmers can become accustomed to the situation and help them to gain confidence. It is also possible to start a group with the faster swimmers lining up in the water behind slower swimmers and then trying to swim their way through to the front. If this practice session is used from the deep end of the pool, it also gives some idea of deep-water starts where the starting line is out from the beach or lakeside and swimmers need to tread water before they begin.

Training to tread water

It is worth training on a breaststroke-type frog kick action to stay afloat, with the legs working non-simultaneously. This prevents bobbing up and down and also gives a little more space as others will move away from flailing legs.

If you come from a swimming background and feel confident, you should attempt to maximize your strengths and get a good start. This fast start will create an oxygen debt which you need to be aware of, and be prepared to deal with a feeling of extreme breathlessness soon after the start. As the pace settles down, this oxygen debt will go. You can train specifically to improve the high-intensity fitness needed for a swim sprint, which simultaneously gets you used to the feeling of breathlessness. This can be done in the pool as follows:

- fast repetition swims with little rest
- sprint swims over short distances using breath-holding
- simulating the conditions by swimming time trials with the first 50, 100 or 200 metres flat-out, and then holding on to the race pace.

Training like this is particularly effective before your first event.

Mid- and end-race

After the start you will be able to settle into your stroke and take advantage of legal drafting (see below). Remember that the major difference between swimming in a triathlon and swimming as an individual sport is that you have to cycle and run after your swim section. It is much better to conserve energy during this phase of the swim and concentrate on your stroke technique. Be aware of swimmers around you and keep checking that you're swimming in a straight line rather than just following somebody's feet; after all, they may be swimming far from straight.

Drafting during the swim

Drafting occurs when you closely follow another athlete. It is permitted during the swim and the run, but not permitted in age group competition in the cycling discipline. During cycling, resistance to frontal resistance (usually wind) is negated, meaning that the following cyclist has to exert far less effort for a similar speed. This also occurs on the run but to a lesser extent because running speeds are so much less than in cycling.

The drafting effect when following closely behind another swimmer makes a massive difference in exertion during this phase of the race as the resistance of still water to any mass moving through it is huge. As it is allowed during triathlons it can make big differences to your speed in the water and the amount of effort required. Saving energy means that you can move into transition and the bike phase feeling fresh. It is essential that you practise drafting regularly during training in preparation for open water swims.

Are you a drafter?

Many swimmers already draft during swimming training sessions without realizing that is what it is called. As swimmers become more fatigued during the session, they will instinctively move closer to the swimmer in front. In most swimming training sessions, swimmers will go off with a three- or five-second gap between themselves and the swimmer in front. It is a natural reaction to push away from the wall a little early and get immediately behind the swimmer in front. Trying to swim as near as possible to the front swimmer's toes is a drafting effect called 'sitting on the feet'. Frequently a swimmer using this technique will find it necessary to slow down rather than swim into the preceding swimmer's feet.

Swimming slightly to the side of the swimmer in front achieves the slipstreaming effect and demonstrates the difference in effort used when drafting; the swimmer in front works hard, the swimmer following cruises. Swimming coaches are well aware of this, of course, and will make swimmers rotate the lead so that nobody has an easy ride throughout any one session. This works extremely well for triathletes, and incorporating drafting into a training session allows everyone to experience the effect of this type of work by sharing the lead. The familiarity of doing this in training will also ensure that athletes know how to use drafting to their advantage and also learn how and when to 'back-off' so they don't infringe on the swimmer in front by continually touching their feet.

Because following a swimmer is faster than leading, the leading swimmer can wear hand paddles and use a pull buoy. Most swimmers are faster when wearing these and the drafting swimmer will need to work hard to keep up. In this way a good training session is assured for all swimmers.

Hip drafting

As well as drafting on the feet of the swimmer in front, it is also possible to draft on the hip of the swimmer in front. In a big swimming pack in open water it may not be feasible to draft directly off a swimmer's feet, however, there is still a considerable drafting effect from the hips, and this also allows a drafting swimmer to see more easily. In open water there can be a feeling of panic when drafting immediately behind someone, as visibility can be poor in the bubbles and white water generated by the legs and feet kick.

Swim training to improve open water swimming

Although training sessions will help towards any racing swim, they really improve open water swimming as they help you to:

- swim fast at the start to escape the pack of swimmers
- swim faster so that you can catch up with a swimmer and benefit from drafting
- practise drafting – training in groups in a pool without lane ropes can quickly teach triathletes to use whichever mode of drafting is the best in any particular circumstances.

Swimming training sessions also simulate the feelings of discomfort that are felt during a triathlon, but although it is demanding, it will pay dividends in performance and may be the difference between simply 'getting through' that first race and actually enjoying it. You will only realize how important these sessions have been sometime during that first race, and you will then be relieved that you have done them.

Learning how to swim fast

Drafting on someone faster creates less effort and a faster time, but learning how to do this in practice, to maintain contact with a faster swimmer right from the start, is a little more difficult; you need to learn how to get that early speed. The speed doesn't need to be maintained for a long time as, when drafting, less effort is required at any speed. The only way to become proficient at flat-out, fast-starting swimming is to practise it. Simulate that flat-out start which is required from the gun to stick to the feet of your target, the swimmer that you know will drag you around just so long as you can maintain contact. This flat-out swimming practice is also good practice if you want to get away from a crowd of swimmers into clearer water.

Simulating the start of the swim

A triathlon swim-specific session should have a very fast initial period and then almost immediately relax into the pace that you intend to maintain for the rest of the swim discipline. The session below is a very demanding session, but it simulates the typical triathlon swim. After the initial warm-up:

1 swim 100 metres flat-out, rest for ten seconds then
2 swim 100 metres at race pace, rest for 30 seconds
3 swim 100 metres flat-out, rest for ten seconds then
4 swim 200 metres at race pace, rest for 30 seconds
5 swim 100 metres flat-out, rest for ten seconds then
6 swim 300 metres at race pace, rest for 30 seconds
7 swim 100 metres flat-out, rest for ten seconds then
8 swim 400 metres at race pace.

Now this is an extremely tough session of 1400 metres in all, but what it does do is to give you that exact feeling of how hard the swim start is, and the feeling of holding race pace when you're tired from that explosive start. Remember that your current state of fitness dictates how much you can do during a session, and it may well be that you will want to miss the fourth and final explosive 100 metres and the final race pace of 400 metres when you begin. If you still feel that you have a lot of work to do on swimming but realize that this type of session does work, you might want to start with less distance. It remains important that the intensity is high. The session would then look like this:

1 swim 50 metres flat-out, rest for ten seconds only then
2 swim 50 metres at race pace, rest for 30 seconds
3 swim 50 metres flat-out, rest for ten seconds only then
4 swim 100 metres at race pace, rest for 30 seconds
5 swim 50 metres flat-out, rest for ten seconds only then
6 swim 150 metres at race pace, rest for 30 seconds
7 swim 50 metres flat-out, rest for ten seconds only then
8 swim 200 metres at race pace.

The total distance covered is still 700 metres, and for many new triathletes who are starting with a sprint distance event where the swim is 750 metres, this is adequate.

Learning how to draft

If you have managed a good fast start, then you must take advantage of the faster swimmers at the front of the pack. Practising drafting during training can be done during a pool session by using the swimmer in front, staying as close to the swimmer as possible, 'sitting on the feet' and trying to swim about four to six inches off the swimmer's toes.

Alternatively, pair up with a friend who is also just starting triathlon or swimming training (or a triathlete with some experience). The swimmer in front can wear hand-paddles and use a pull buoy. However, by ensuring that the following/drafting swimmer gets immediately onto the feet of the leader the advantage of wearing the paddles is negated and the drafting effect can be seen to be working efficiently.

Differences in stroke and technique

There are a number of key differences between swimming in a pool, and taking to the open water.

Wetsuits

Wetsuits are an advantage, particularly for the weaker swimmer, as they add buoyancy. New triathletes would be advised to wear them when water temperature allows (in cold temperatures they are compulsory), but wetsuits can be uncomfortable at first, even with the excellent standards of comfort and flexibility that most wetsuits now possess. Wetsuits need to be tight, without that they would not be doing their job. Wetsuit manufacturers have researched and developed extremely flexible and buoyant wetsuits so that your open water swimming is comfortable and improved.

Benefits of a wetsuit
- They maintain a better body temperature.
- With a well-fitted wetsuit you can significantly improve your swim time because of reduced drag and improved buoyancy.

Possible drawbacks of a wetsuit
- A badly-fitted wetsuit will fill with water and create more drag.

- Shoulder movement may feel a little restricted when wearing a wetsuit. To overcome this lack of mobility, you will need to emphasize the shoulder roll more.
- Feelings of tightness in the chest may also be exaggerated by wearing a wetsuit, so a good fit is essential.

As you can see, any drawbacks can be overcome by a good fit and good swimming technique. Swimming in a wetsuit changes your body position, but you should not need to change the mechanics of a good stroke technique. Any changes will be subtle and are likely to be to breathing pattern and lessening the leg kick. The extra buoyancy provided by the neoprene lifts the legs, and a very shallow leg kick with minimal knee bend will maintain the flat body position. A two-beat leg kick with good ankle flexibility needs to be maintained. Hyperextension (pointing) of the toes will also reduce drag. It is important to remember that cycling and running is still to come and it is necessary to have the leg muscles rested rather than exhausted after the swim.

As you approach the end of the swim, mentally prepare for your transition (see Chapter 08). Again, be aware of the swimmers near to you and make sure that you have a clear exit from the swim and into the swim/cycle transition area.

Sighting and swimming straight

The ability to swim in a straight line is largely taken care of in a swimming pool by having a painted blue or black line to follow on the bottom of the pool. This does not occur in a lake or the sea. Sighting is not so easy outdoors but is an essential part of open water swimming. The ability to swim straight between the marker buoys will ensure that you keep your actual swimming distance as close as possible to the race distance. The athlete can practise this straight-line swimming and sighting in a number of ways.

Water polo drill

Water polo is sometimes called 'basketball in water with American football rules'. If you have seen a water polo match you will understand. Water polo players need to be able to swim with their heads out of the water so that they can follow the water polo ball and sight the field of play. This creates a high head position with hyperextension of the neck, and can cause an aching sensation if held too long. Lifting the head also unbalances the effective neutral flat body position by pushing the legs lower, so it should not be overdone. Lifting the head enough so that you can see in front will keep you moving in a straight line. Try not to breathe to the front during this movement, but maintain your normal breathing pattern.

Practising the water polo drill

It would be impossible and inadvisable (and slow) to attempt to swim an entire open water race like this, so it is important to use 20–30 normal swimming strokes before lifting the head up for six water polo strokes in training. It is better to lift for six strokes because lifting for just two or three to resume a flat body position sooner is not likely to give enough time to sight properly. There may well be water streaming over your goggles, and the goggles could be slightly fogged. Also in dull, overcast conditions two or three 'water polo' strokes will not be enough time to take a proper look ahead.

Swimming with eyes closed

Eyes-closed swimming has limitations as it can only be done over short distances and can only be done by a few swimmers at any one time. The drill can be done either in a clear pool or in a single lane. With eyes open, swim one length of the pool in a straight line (follow the black line) and count the number of strokes in one length. Swim as you would expect in a race with a controlled stroke and technique. Do this again with eyes closed, imagining you are swimming over the black line. Some swimmers may swim diagonally from one side of the pool to the other if no lane ropes are set out; if lane ropes are in place the swimmer may bounce from one lane rope to the other. Some swimmers will practise this by putting cotton wool in their swimming goggles.

There are a number of reasons why this non-straight line happens:

- Sense of direction is easily lost if you take away familiar surroundings.
- Both arms need to be pulling equally hard and in parallel directions to maintain a straight line.
- Body roll may be different from side to side.

Why swim with eyes closed?

- It might highlight any imbalances in body roll, or in arm strength or technique.
- It gets you used to swimming without being able to see, which can occur with fogged-up goggles.
- It enables you to practise short stretches of swimming with your eyes closed, which may be useful when in the midst of lots of other swimmers and white water.

Bilateral breathing

This helps balance the swimming stroke and ensures that you are comfortable in an open water triathlon race, whatever the conditions. The ability and skill to be able to choose to breathe to the left or right, away from glaring sunshine, lashing rain or big waves, is invaluable. It is necessary to be prepared for any conditions in open water swimming: rain and wind direction; tide and current conditions; height and direction of waves; and surf. All these can affect your confidence, even if you are a strong swimmer. In these situations it is essential that you are able to locate key points for sighting.

The ability and confidence of breathing on both sides (bilateral breathing) goes some way to overcoming difficulties in these situations. It is an essential skill in triathlon, not only for a more balanced technique and flat body position, but to allow the triathlete to see what and who is around during the swim. Introducing bilateral breathing into training sessions is often initially difficult – breaths are taken every three strokes rather than every two – but this quickly becomes an accepted part of training. Attempting to breathe to both sides in some part of all swimming training sessions will help balance the stroke and make better use of the powerful muscle groups in the back and shoulders rather than just the arm muscles. A bilateral breathing pattern also contributes to swimming straight.

Top tip

Training using the catch-up technique (see Chapter 04) while wearing fins will aid bilateral breathing. Breathing on every stroke on alternate sides as each arm is held in front of the head is good training for bilateral breathing.

Bilateral breathing may help to correct some technique faults, such as:

- lateral deviation (snaking)
- arms entering over the centre line of the head
- too much shoulder rotation.

Holding your breath

Working on bilateral breathing in training will also make breath-holding easier. Breath-holding may be necessary in certain conditions:

- rough water
- when large waves are coming in from the side
- when you need to move quickly away from a pack of swimmers that is threatening to envelop you.

Once breathing every two strokes has progressed to bilateral breathing (every three strokes), this should be further progressed by breathing one length using the normal breathing pattern and then one length breathing every four strokes, and gradually increasing to five or six. It must be emphasized that breath-holding is not recommended for normal swimming in pleasant conditions; it is tiring and will quickly lead to breathlessness, oxygen debt and a falling away of technique. However, it is a skill that needs to be available when conditions dictate.

T-shirt training

Occasionally wearing a T-shirt during training causes drag and resistance, and can be used during training sessions. Changes in body position, breathing and the extra effort required to swim well are created by wearing a T-shirt, and will help a lot in adjusting to open water conditions. As with breath-holding, wearing a T-shirt for training sessions (preferably only for a part of a session) should be used infrequently and only so that the swimmer feels confident swimming in adverse conditions.

Safety aspects

Swimming in open water is dangerous. In swimming pools there are lifeguards, lane ropes and pool edges; there is always something or someone to help, and you are always able to take a rest if needed. In open water these safety aspects are not available. Never swim alone, and always wear a bright swim cap so you are easily visible.

Racing strategies for open water swimming

In addition to the drills in this chapter which will particularly benefit open water swimming, there are a number of strategies you can employ to maximize your open water swim and swim-cycle transition.

1 It will save transition time if you wear everything you plan to race in under your wetsuit, including your race number either pinned to a top or onto a piece of elastic. Putting a dry top over a wet body is extremely frustrating and time-consuming (see Chapter 08 for tips on transition).

2 Be prepared for any weather conditions. Having two pairs of goggles at the race in case of bright sunny (dark or tinted pair) or overcast conditions (clear or light-coloured pair) ensures that you are prepared.

3 Some triathletes place the strap of their swimming goggles underneath their swim hat. If the goggles are inadvertently hit by another competitor, the swim hat will keep the goggles in position.

4 Race smart. A fast swim start or a cautious one? Race to your strengths, don't think that you will overcome any weaknesses during the race – this is best done in training.

5 Check out the course before the race so you are familiar with it.

6 Is it better to be on one side of the main pack than the other? The straightest route to the first buoy might not be advisable if it means swimming directly against a stronger current or bigger waves in a sea swim.

7 Walk the route from swim exit to your bike a few times to get familiar with landmarks around the exit. Ensure that you use a fixed object to mark your route. Cars and boats can move!

8 Changing direction during an open water swim usually means turning around large buoys. This may be intimidating, particularly at the first turning buoy where there will be a lot of swimmers converging, and weaker swimmers will be pushed sideways and outwards or even pushed under. Strategies include:
   • going wide
   • getting ahead
   • hanging back and then moving up.

Top tip

It is also advisable to practise turning onto your back for one stroke as you go round the buoy. This 360° rotation will bring you closer to the buoy and save a little time and distance.

So with the swim tied up, let's look at the next discipline – the cycle.

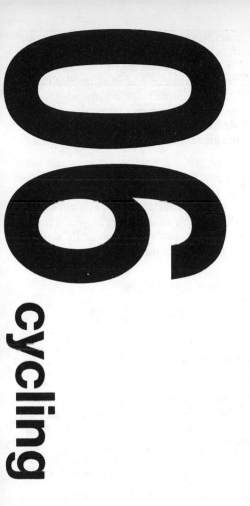

06

cycling

In this chapter you will learn:
- how to set up and adjust your bike for the perfect riding position
- the mechanics of the bicycle
- the correct pedalling technique
- bike handling skills
- about training programmes.

Cycling is the single discipline in triathlon where good equipment can make a difference to performance. This does not mean that the bike needs to be expensive; it is more important that it is the correct size for the athlete and it is mechanically sound. It is essential that the bike and rider complement each other perfectly, combining comfort and mechanical efficiency, good aerodynamics, and flexibility of changing riding position so the athlete can cope with all racing and training conditions.

After reading this chapter you will be able to set up your bike (or any bike) for a perfect riding position for you – essential for comfort, speed and good aerodynamics. You'll learn how big a bike frame should be, what rpm (revolutions per minute) to ride at, and how to know whether you're in the correct gear. Finally, the information on bike handling and pedalling drills will set you up to sail through the cycling training programmes at the end of this chapter.

The riding position – setting up correctly

Cycling has to overcome three main forces:

- **Air resistance** – as you cycle, the wind hits you and slows you down, so reducing resistance is essential.
- **Friction** – the tyres rolling on the road surface – ensure that your tyres are pumped up to the recommended level for the road surface and weather.
- **Gravity** – riding up hills – it is essential that your bike is set up properly and that your riding position is perfect.

Cyclists go to great lengths to ensure that their riding position is absolutely correct for them as individuals. There are a number of general rules that apply to setting the correct position, but each individual will have their own specific position that applies to them and ensures that they will get maximum force, power and fluidity of movement during cycle training and racing. The points of contact between the cyclist and the bike are:

- saddle and backside
- pedals and feet
- handlebars and hands.

Bike and saddle height

The height of the saddle is vitally important and should be set first.

1 Sit on the saddle and place the left crank at the bottom of the stroke in line with the seat tube.

2 Place the heel of the foot (wear the cycling or training shoes that you will normally ride in) onto the pedal. The leg should be almost straight but not overstretched. If you are wearing cycling shoes, don't forget to add on thickness of the shoe plate that clips into the pedal.

Top tip

How big should your bike be? A general rule for bike frame size is to take two-thirds of the inside leg measurement. For example, a rider with a 32-inch inside leg would need a 21-inch frame size.

Forward and back saddle position

With saddle height set, and after making sure that the saddle is level (parallel to the ground and the bike's top tube), you are ready to check the forward and backward position of the saddle to ensure that you are not too stretched out nor too bunched up.

1 Sit on the saddle with your cycling shoes on and clipped into the pedals.

2 Place the pedals in a horizontal position (the chainwheel cranks should be 'flat'), and check that your knee is directly above the ball of the foot while clipped into the pedal. If the knee is not above the foot, adjust the saddle forwards or backwards until it is.

3 Your fingertips should just touch or be a fraction behind the back edge of the handlebars. It is possible to replace the handlebar stem with one of a different length if this is necessary for an optimum riding position. If there is a big change in the forward and back position, it may be necessary to readjust the saddle height.

Handlebars

With the essential height and forward positions fixed, now turn your attention to the handlebars.

1 Set the handlebars so that the bottom of the bars, where they flatten out, are parallel to the top tube.
2 Now set the brake levers ensuring they are facing directly forwards and not tilting either too much up or down.

> **Top tip**
>
> The height of the top of the handlebars should be between roughly level and five centimetres below the top of the saddle when you begin riding, but will gradually drop down as you become more confident. However, the handlebar height will depend on the flexibility of the rider. You must be comfortable with your hands on the drop position (bottom of the handlebars), and on the top of the handlebars, and it must be easy for you to reach the brakes.

Adjusting your bike

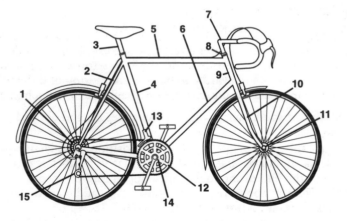

1 Free wheel gear cluster	**9** Head tube
2 Seat stays	**10** Front forks
3 Seat pin	**11** Hub/quick release
4 Seat tube	**12** Chainwheel
5 Top tube	**13** Front derailleur
6 Down tube	**14** Bottom bracket
7 Handlebar stem	**15** Rear derailleur
8 Headset	

figure 6.1 bicycle parts

In the first instance, take advice from a mechanic in a cycle shop, but by listening and learning, you should soon be able to adjust the bike to suit your height, leg length and riding position. Instructions for setting up bike positions are only guidelines and must allow for individual preferences, strengths and weaknesses. If you change riding and set-up positions for any reason, make these changes gradually, as attempting to make too big a change may cause soreness and injury.

Modern bikes have a great range of adjustments, and bike size (within reasonable parameters) is not critical. Easy adjustments can be made as follows:

- saddle height
- saddle front and rear position
- handlebar height
- stem length, affecting handlebar forward and back position.

Bike maintenance

Having a clean bike is important, not just for esoteric reasons, but primarily so that any structural and mechanical faults are not hidden by dirt. You should methodically check the frame, wheels and tyres, freewheel and chain, brakes, headset, handlebars and stem, gears, chainwheel and bottom bracket, and pedals on a regular basis.

Frame
- Check for cracks all over but particularly where the frame tubes join each other.

Wheels
- Check for buckling, kinks and dents in the rim.
- Check the wheel hubs for any grinding noises that will indicate wear and dirt in the bearings.
- Check spokes for tightness and signs of wear where they meet the hubs. Most wheel hubs now have a 'quick release' mechanism which does exactly what it says. Take out the quick-release spindle from the hubs and clean it. Lightly grease it and put it back. On the rear hub check that the gear sprockets on the right-hand side are spinning in line with the hub and wheel. You will need the wheel off the frame for this check.

Tyres

- Check the tread for cuts, small holes and bald patches.
- Check the undercord (a layer that goes between the inner tube and the inside of the wheel rim) for fraying – unless these are minor, replace the tyre.
- Any bulges or deep cuts in the tyres indicate that they should be replaced.

Freewheel and chain

- Any dirt here will gradually wear down the metal chain and freewheel block; they must be kept clean.
- The chain should be tense but not overtight.
- Be aware of any stiff links or tiny cracks in the chain.
- Clean between the teeth of the freewheel using an old rag to pull the dirt out – the freewheel should spin freely and noiselessly.
- The chain and freewheel should always be clean and lightly oiled.

Brakes

The brakes **must** work efficiently.

- Ensure that brake blocks are not worn out.
- Check that the brake cables are free-running and responsive so that there is an immediate reaction when pulling on the brakes.
- The cables must be kept oiled and not be frayed.
- The brake unit must be central over and around the wheel rim so braking is smooth.

Headset, handlebars and stem

- The bolt locking the handlebars to the stem must be completely tight.
- The headset must be able to turn the full range smoothly – if the headset self-centres, it is an indication that the bearings inside are worn or pitted and may cause the headset to lock.
- Any looseness in the headset also indicates worn bearings. It is essential to replace worn bearings immediately.

Gears

- Gears must be free-running, with the chain going up and down across each gear and sprocket smoothly and staying in the required gear.
- Ensure that after any gear adjustment that all the gears are available.

Chainwheel and bottom bracket

- The teeth on the chainwheel must also be checked for wear.
- The chainwheel must be free-running and spin easily. Most bottom bracket units are now sealed and there should not be any tightness or lateral movement in the bracket. However, in some older bikes the bearings can become worn and cause stiffness that will create friction against the pedalling action, or make the chainwheel so loose with lateral movement that it is dangerous.

Pedals

- Pedals must be free-spinning and tightened safely to the cranks.
- Cleats attach your feet firmly to the pedals allowing you to introduce more power and control throughout the full cycle of the pedal.

Pedalling and pedalling drills

Pedalling is a circular action but new cyclists and triathletes will instinctively pedal in a piston-type, up-and-down action. It is essential to train so that you start pedalling in the smoother circular action. Circular pedalling places a more equal load on different muscle groups, spreading out muscular demands and delaying fatigue. This is crucial for triathletes who must run after the bike section. However, circular pedalling does not mean that equal pressure will be applied throughout the entire pedalling movement.

Correct pedal power

It is important to maintain or increase the power on the piston up and down movement while at the same time improving circular movement cycling efficiency. To increase power and efficiency, push the pedals **across the top** of the pedal stroke circle – this creates a longer power stroke by starting the application of force before the down stroke begins, and keeps that force on the pedal throughout the majority of each revolution. We should also pedal in a direction that is 90° to the crank arm.

Push turns into pull through the bottom of the pedal stroke. This maintains a constant force through the entire pedalling circle and balances the opposite leg pushing at the top of the pedal stroke. A slight lift of the foot off the pedal as the pedal comes up at the rear also helps to balance and save energy. With the foot resting on the pedal, more resistance is created for the leg that is pushing down on the other pedal. Pulling up with great force is not necessary, just lifting slightly will suffice. Lift your knee as if you're walking up steep stairs or stepping onto a box. As discussed with swimming drills, don't attempt everything at the same time. Focus on one aspect of efficient pedalling before moving on to the next. Again, as with swimming, put 'the full stroke' together in between the drills.

Top tip

When practising drills for cycling, it is recommended that you use a turbo trainer or wind trainer (see Chapter 02). Cycling on the road always has inherent danger and when practising new drills, attention can be focused on the drill.

The pedal cycle

Use a picture of a clock face to master the perfect revolution and to determine how and where pedal force should be applied to the pedal.

Time on clock face	Pedal position
12 o'clock	Top of the pedal stroke – move the pedal forwards.
2 o'clock	Move the pedal slightly forward and down.
3 o'clock	Push directly down.
4 o'clock	Move the pedal slightly back and down.
6 o'clock	Pull the pedal backwards.

The power phase (scraping off the shoe)

Imagine that you have stepped in a very unpleasant substance that is now on the bottom of your cycling shoe. As you approach the 5 o'clock position, rotate the ankle as if you are scraping the shoe. Maintain this scrape and rotation to the 7 o'clock position. This will increase the length of the power phase.

Up and through

As your foot comes up the pull phase towards 11 o'clock, imagine kicking forward hard with the toes up. Push and kick your foot over the top as if trying to begin the push phase a little earlier. This will increase the length of the power phase by beginning the power push earlier.

Overcoming dead spots

The least efficient phases of pedalling are the two at the top and bottom of the circle, between 6 and 7 o'clock and between 12 and 2 o'clock. If you concentrate on your legs moving and changing throughout the entire circle you will maintain greater power; this will combine with the earlier drills and overcome the dead spots.

Single leg pedalling

Pedalling with one leg will emphasize and exaggerate any faults in the pedal action, whereas pedalling with both legs will cover up any weak or dead spots as the leg in the push position compensates for the leg pulling. Try this:

1 Rest one leg on a chair placed next to the turbo trainer.
2 Select an easy gear and start pedalling with one leg.
3 You will be aware very quickly if you have chosen too big a gear as your upper leg muscles will fatigue very quickly.
4 Don't use too small a gear as easy momentum will circle the pedal up over the top.
5 Keep the legs relaxed and smooth.
6 Pedal right-legged for one minute, then switch to the left leg and repeat five times.

It takes a lot of effort to pull through the bottom of the pedal stroke and lift the pedal back up and over the top. Focus on eliminating the dead spots at the bottom and top of the pedalling cycle, and keep the pedalling motion as even and smooth as possible. This will be difficult at first but improvements are quick on this drill. If there is change in the sound and noise of the tyre on the rollers, it is probable that there is not a constant and efficient circling motion.

Cadence (speed) and leg speed

Most cyclists ride at between 85 and 105 revolutions per minute (rpm). However, everyone is different, and you may be at the top or bottom of the range. This drill will help you develop cadence (pedalling speed), but you should also test yourself on a measured course in different gears and see how cadence affects your speed.

1 Select an easy gear and start pedalling, gradually increase cadence (speed of pedalling) until it is difficult to keep still on the saddle and you will feel as if you're bouncing up and down.
2 Gradually bring the cadence down until you stop bouncing and maintain that cadence for between 15 to 30 seconds.
3 Slow down cadence until you recover and then repeat.
4 Try to keep the pedalling action smooth and relaxed throughout.

As with the single leg drill, any change in the sound and noise of the tyre on the rollers means an inefficient pedalling action.

As with all drills, concentrate on doing them properly at a slow speed to begin with, then increase the speed. With cycling it is important that you attempt these drills in the position on the bike that you will be racing in – your racing position. This will normally mean with your hands at the bottom of the handlebars.

Top tip

It's important to use your gears to create the right revs per minute. Try to relax when riding and don't push 'big' gears. You should be trying to achieve 90 to 100 revolutions per minute. If your pedal revolutions per minute are less than 80, you are probably in too big a gear. Similarly, if you are pedalling more than 100 revolutions per minute, your gearing is probably too easy. Pushing big gears fatigues you quickly and makes it difficult to run well after the cycle.

Strength work

There is a need for strength and power as fitness progresses on the bike discipline. There is still a need to emphasize the circular pedalling action, even though the cadence will necessarily be slower whilst you do this. Select a big, challenging gear that you can pedal at 60 to 70 rpm, stay in this gear for one minute, then select an easy gear and pedal at 100 rpm or more for two minutes. Repeat five to six times.

Bike handling skills

Changing gear

The secret to smooth gear changing is to plan ahead. Be ready for hills and change into an easier gear earlier than you think you will need to, this is particularly important for hills, as you will lose momentum as soon as you start climbing. You must keep pedalling as you change gear and maintain pressure on the pedals.

Maintaining speed through turns and corners

Try to keep your momentum up through turns. Applying the brakes when there is no need means that you have to use a lot of energy to get back up to speed after the turn. New riders are usually very cautious and will do this often. Try to do the following instead:

1 Change down a gear before the turn.
2 Stop pedalling.
3 Now lean the bike into the corner.

Again, new riders are cautious of leaning the bike. Be assured there is little danger here. Cornering and turning do reduce speed, and standing as you come out of the turn and pedalling hard will regain the speed more quickly. A lot of energy is used when standing on the pedals so be cautious about this.

Controlling speed

If you find you are going too fast into a turn, you must lean into the curve – it's better to increase your cornering angle.

1 Put your weight on the outside (of the turn) pedal (this will give the tyres more grip).
2 Brake early rather than late – putting on the brakes at the end of a turn will tend to straighten out the bike, which is the opposite of what you need it to do.
3 Light braking on the rear wheel can help, but if it catches and seizes, release immediately.
4 Do not use your front brake in a turn; the front wheel will slide away.

Sighting, steering, direction and control

Don't only look directly in front of your front wheel. Look further ahead and check the whole corner before you enter it. Be aware of the best riding line all the way through the corner and follow it. Your bike will go where you look. Even when riding in a straight line, focus ahead and don't look down at the front wheel; looking too close means correcting line and control, and is unsafe.

Confidence and group riding

Riding in a group quickly instils confidence, and group riding on long training endurance rides is recommended. To begin with, ride at a relatively slow speed with a smooth pedal action one rider behind the other with a gap of about a metre or so. Riders should aim for similar cadence by choosing a similar gear. To avoid freewheeling, this drill can be performed on a gentle slope. Riders will learn to be confident by following and if anything does go wrong, it is easy just to put a foot down on the ground.

As confidence increases, two lines can be formed instead of one so the rider has someone beside as well as in front and behind. You should aim to gradually close the gap between yourself and the rider in front of you, and change positions as follows:

- Take turns at the front of the line by the lead rider checking over their shoulder for any danger, moving to one side and slowing the cadence slightly.
- The next rider takes the lead not by accelerating but by maintaining speed as the previous lead rider gradually goes back down the line.
- You should stay close as you pass the other riders while rotating the lead.
- As you drop towards the back of the line, accelerate slightly as your front wheel is next to the back rider's rear wheel. This will give you the slight impetus needed to move in immediately without letting a gap open.

Training for cycling in triathlon

There is no substitute for just getting out and riding on the road to begin cycling training. Endurance and stamina along with confidence will build up. It's best to start with short rides and gradually increase the time spent riding. Importantly, don't choose to ride in big gears, especially to start with; instead, spin the pedals easily and aim for a cadence of 90 rpm plus. As with swimming and running, there is a suggested six-month training schedule in Chapter 11. However, an absolute beginner who is able to train three times each week on the bike might have a schedule similar to the one below. The blank days are either rest days or for swimming and/or running training, although you may opt to include training for these disciplines with your cycling training, as shown in Chapter 11.

Eight-week cycling training programme

	MON	TUES	WED	THURS	FRI	SAT	SUN
WEEK 1	30 mins ride		45 min ride			turbo session	
WEEK 2	30 mins ride increase pace gradually every 10 mins				1 hour ride		turbo session
WEEK 3	30 mins ride		1 hour ride (20 mins easy, 20 mins hard, 20 mins average)			turbo session	
WEEK 4	30 mins ride		1 hour turbo session				
WEEK 5			45 mins hard ride		1 hour steady ride		turbo session

	MON	TUES	WED	THURS	FRI	SAT	SUN
WEEK 6	45 mins steady ride		1 hour hard ride			turbo session	
WEEK 7	turbo session				1 hour steady ride		1 hour hard ride
WEEK 8			1 hour steady ride		1 hour hard ride		turbo session

Turbo training

Training on the turbo/wind trainer is a simple way to complete drill training and introduce interval training into your schedule without taking any risks due to road or traffic conditions. A beginner might have their eight weeks of sessions becoming progressively more demanding as below. All sessions should take account of the following guidelines:

• Focus on good pedalling technique.
• Train in your racing position.
• Aim for a cadence of 90 plus.
• Each session should have an easy ten minutes of spin pedalling to warm-up and to warm-down.

An extra variety that can be introduced into cycle training is the appropriate use of the gears. Most front chainwheels will have between 49 and 53 teeth on the larger outside ring, and between 36 and 46 teeth on the smaller inside ring. The gear sprockets will have between 12 and 15 teeth on the smallest sprocket and between 18 and 27 teeth on the largest sprocket.

The sessions below are examples only, and triathletes should choose the appropriate gear ratio. However, the sessions should be progressive with the gearing becoming more demanding over the eight-week period. These training sessions involving use of different gears and cadence should be incorporated into an overall weekly cycling training plan similar to the one shown opposite.

figure 6.2 chainwheel and sprockets

Gear training to be incorporated into cycle training sessions

WEEK 1	7 repetitions of 52 × 20 for 1 minute at 90 to 100 rpm. Recovery – 42 × 20 for 1 minute at 60 rpm.
WEEK 2	5 repetitions of 52 × 20 for 2 minutes at 90 to 100 rpm. Recovery – 42 × 20 for 1 minute at 60 rpm.
WEEK 3	6 reps of 52 × 18 for 2 mins 90–100 rpm. Recovery – 42 × 20 for 1 min at 60 rpm.
WEEK 4	6 repetitions of 52 × 20 for 3 minutes at 90 to 100 rpm. Recovery – 42 × 20 for 1 minute at 60 rpm.
WEEK 5	8 repetitions of 52 × 18 for 2 minutes at 90 to 100 rpm. Recovery – 42 × 20 for 1 minute at 60 rpm.
WEEK 6	4 repetitions of 52 × 18 for 4 minutes at 90 to 100 rpm. Recovery – 42 × 20 for 2 minutes at 60 rpm.
WEEK 7	6 repetitions of 52 × 16 for 3 minutes at 90 to 100 rpm. Recovery – 42 × 20 for 2 minutes at 60 rpm.
WEEK 8	3 repetitions of 52 × 18 for 5 minutes at 90 to 100 rpm. Recovery – 42 × 20 for 2 minutes at 60 rpm.

The progressive eight sessions fit all the criteria that is required and should ensure that the new triathlete increases fitness along with pedalling technique and cadence.

Before you learn how to have an effective transition between the cycle and the run, let's take a look at the final discipline of running.

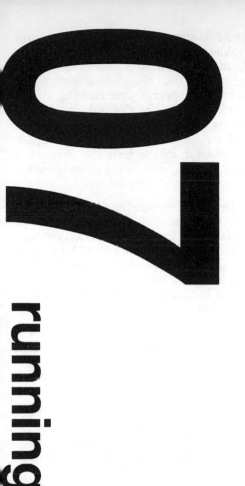

07

running

In this chapter you will learn:
- how to run correctly with good technique
- drills to improve your running technique and speed
- the differences between running as a single discipline and running in a triathlon
- about running schedules and training sessions.

The big difference between running as an individual sport, and running as the final discipline of a triathlon is that in triathlon running, you are already tired from having swam and cycled, and you bring that fatigue into the final discipline. It is very easy (but wrong) to think and even accept that your running will be much slower and something to endure as a misery rather than something to be enjoyed. As well as the extra fatigue that is present from running and swimming (some athletes compare running in a triathlon as similar to the final six miles of a marathon), it is the nature of cycling that makes running such a challenge initially.

In cycling your legs have been circling continually without any pounding on the ground. Mentally, you are attuned to this movement. Then the run starts and the circular motion changes to an up-and-down one, and crucially the impact of hitting the ground each time creates stress and muscle trauma. Running experts believe that as the weight of the body is carried by the legs, the impact each time of hitting the ground multiplies that weight by as much as four times.

Even if you come from a running background, there are no short cuts in becoming a good runner in a triathlon; technique, speed, strength and mobility all play their part – along with the knowledge that triathlon running is different and has extra specific requirements to race well.

This chapter outlines the basics of good running technique – essential to enjoy injury-free running and get those miles in! Working through the running drills will help fine-tune your technique and enable you to increase your running speed – even after getting off your bike.

Running technique

It is a popular misconception that running is a purely 'natural' activity and that we don't need to spend any time practising the technique. This is wrong. Not only will a poor technique slow you down and prevent you from reaching your potential, it will also lead to injuries and a shortening of an active sporting life. As with swimming and cycling, no time spent on running technique is wasted. Correct running technique will ultimately make you run faster.

For any runner to perform at their best it is important that they run efficiently, allowing their body to use as little energy as possible on each step, whilst maintaining the required stride length and cadence.

To improve your time you must lengthen your stride (caution required here), increase your cadence, or both, using a combination of improved strength, fitness and running technique. Although a good stride length is important, it must be stressed that attempting to stretch or lengthen stride length artificially will slow your running speed down and can easily cause injury. Too long a stride length means that the body weight will be behind the feet each time as they touch the ground, creating a 'braking' effect. It can also lead to sore muscles and injury.

Basically, in running,

speed = stride length × stride rate

To improve either of these factors, we must increase the range of movement in the joints and the strength in the running muscle groups. However, before we look at technique for the lower body, let's briefly consider the position of the upper body.

The upper body and arms in a running action

It is also important not to neglect the upper body. Just as a good leg kick in swimming is important for balance and maintaining a good position, a strong upper body and arm drive contributes in running. Take a look at these key points:

- The upper body must stay upright, although a slight full body lean forward can make running easier and faster. However, the lean must be from the feet upwards, never from the hips or above, as this will put a strain on the lower back muscles.
- A powerful, strong arm drive will dictate how fast the legs move and the length of stride. The arm action matches the leg action, with the left arm coming forward at the same time as the right leg and vice versa, in an equal and opposite action and reaction.
- The arm movement should be kept relaxed and rhythmic, moving backwards and forwards in a straight line with the hands loosely cupped and the thumbs resting on the fingers.

The legs in a running action

As in swimming, there is a propulsive phase and a recovery phase in running. As soon as the foot makes contact with the ground, the propulsive phase starts. The body weight is carried by the foot (multiplied by four times, remember) as the hips and trunk pass over the foot, and the hip, knee and ankle stretch out to push the runner forward.

As the foot leaves the ground, recovery begins. The foot is pulled upwards and the thigh swings forward and through until it is almost parallel to the ground. The lower part of the leg then comes forward as the thigh begins to move downwards. The whole leg then sweeps backwards and downwards until the foot strikes the ground again.

There are five basic parts to a running action for the legs that need to be considered. We can break it down further, but essentially they are:

1 toe up
2 heel up
3 knee up
4 reach out
5 claw back.

When we examine these five main factors in leg speed and range of movement we start to realize that it can be extremely difficult to isolate and work on each of these effectively whilst running; therefore, drills become important. We can perform drills to isolate parts of the running action and improve it before putting it all back together as a complete action.

Top tip

The skill of running is maintaining technique under pressure. If this is correct, then the importance of using running drills so that we can maintain that technique when running during a triathlon, after the pressures of swimming and cycling, cannot be over-emphasized. To run fast and efficiently you should have more knee lift, more extension, more claw back and more drive with your arms.

I have emphasized the importance of a good running technique. However, running is essentially a simple basic skill to move forward as fast as possible, and we need to ensure that we don't waste energy by getting away from the forward, horizontal progress by lifting and dropping the head and hips. By always thinking of keeping the hips high, we avoid the body sagging down, particularly as we get progressively more tired, and we don't have to use valuable energy to lift our bodies back up again. In order to maintain good posture whilst running, think of a piece of cotton attached to your head, pulling the head, body and hips upwards.

Good technique versus poor technique

A good runner will have:	A poor runner will have:
an upright running action	a seated running action
almost no vertical movement	body bobs up and down
hips tilted forwards	bottom stuck out
a full body lean from the feet	a lean from the hips or higher
a high knee lift	a low knee lift
a good stride length	an over-long, stretched or very short stride length
a foot strike towards the front of the foot	a heel strike with the foot under or behind the knee
a fast stride frequency (180 steps plus per minute)	a low stride frequency (less than 140 steps per minute)
stride frequency maintained throughout the run	stride frequency slows as tiredness sets in
strong core abdominal muscles	weak abdominal muscles

Common problems

Of course, there are several different ways of running, and although a foot strike on the ball of the foot is deemed to be beneficial to injury prevention and speed, some runners appear to run very easily and very well with a heel-toe strike. It can be very difficult to change your running style if you have been running for a long time, but to ensure that we maintain that good running technique, we must be aware of, and avoid the following:

- **Over-striding** – this creates a braking effect with each stride, reducing momentum and speed.
- **Seated running with hips dropped down and/or backside out** – this detracts from a strong core and can be detrimental to breathing.
- **No neck/tense shoulders** – any tension throughout the body can affect running technique; all muscles except for the core abdominal muscles should be relaxed.
- **A rolling, bobbing head or looking at the road immediately in front of you** – this detracts from good running technique; try to focus on the ground 15–20 feet ahead and relax the jaw. Looking ahead also enables you to plan your footfall and run strategy.
- **Forced or shallow breathing or breath-holding** – a good breathing pattern is essential for aerobic exercise and to relax you; try very deep belly breathing, focusing on breathing out rather than breathing in, or try to create a comfortable breathing pattern in time with every few strides.

Let's take a closer look at elements of running that create common technique problems.

Heel striking

This is usually associated with over-striding and acts as a braking action to your running, as you will be hitting the ground each time in front of your centre of gravity. For every single foot strike you then have to work on getting your weight back over this rather than using the 'claw back' momentum of your foot to propel you forwards. It also increases the stress on joints as you will tend to land heavily.

Leaning backwards

Ideally, your whole body leans slightly forwards (not bending at the waist). Leaning backwards will tend to slow down your running speed, whereas a forward body lean recruits the pull of gravity (as you almost 'fall' forwards) to help increase speed.

To avoid both heel striking and leaning backwards, run tall.

Sideways arm movement

You run forwards, therefore your arms should swing forwards and backwards in the direction you are travelling, not across your body. A little sideways arm movement may often happen to correct some individual anatomical quirk. However, if there is excessive lateral movement you will be twisting your whole body and putting pressure on the lower back and shoulders which may cause injury and joint problems in the long term. The arm action should be economical and relaxed, but the speed and height of the arm swing both at the front and the back will determine the speed at which you are running. It is very easy to slip into a comfort zone as you become more tired during the run and allow the arms to drop.

Top tip

To counteract poor posture and technique, athletes should be encouraged to continually check their running action and do a 'body check' throughout each run. Check head is up and looking slightly ahead, shoulders are down and relaxed, arms relaxed with a forward/backward piston movement, abdominal muscles tight, upright running with full body lean if possible, and forefront foot strike. This should become habitual and should ensure that good technique is maintained however tired you are.

Seated running

Keeping the hips forward and high will ensure that your stride length is good. Seated running where the hips drop is usually caused either by being tired after the cycle section or, more often, by having weak abdominal (core) muscles. Working specifically on the core muscles (see Chapter 03), will ensure that you run tall rather than seated. If you do run seated, it becomes very difficult to maintain a high knee lift that will make a heel strike more likely, and creates very tired muscles in the front of your thighs (quadriceps).

Tired legs

This is a classic triathlon syndrome for the newcomer. It means exactly what it says; your legs are tired after riding the bike, and this tiredness manifests itself in an inability to lift the feet very high off the floor. This can be overcome by mentally focusing on your hamstrings at the back of the upper legs and a mental command to 'lift' after each foot plant. Tired legs mean little knee lift, short stride length and sore hamstrings.

Running drills and skills

There are many different running drills, used for different purposes. This first set of drills is all about getting the brain talking to the feet. They can and should be used in every phase of training and can also be incorporated into the warm-up.

> **Warning**
>
> If you are not used to working on drills or are a newcomer to them, do not try to do too many of them too soon. Your usual range of movement will be extended and the likelihood is that your foot strike will be more powerful. It is worth running on grass as much as possible in the early stages of running drills. While learning new skills, it is likely that the ground impact will be high and soft grass will minimize the chance of injuries.

Warm-up drills

Skipping and hopping

Skipping and hopping are relatively simple drills that require a little coordination. Using skipping and hopping as part of the warm-up will raise the body temperature and warm the muscles, focus on the calf muscles and develop coordination. Essentially, hopping is taking off and landing on the same foot a number of times before repeating the action with the other leg (a short sequence would be left, left, right, right, left, left, right, right), while skipping alternates the foot landed on.

A combination of hopping and skipping is an excellent way to improve coordination and leg strength.

1 Begin with short strides, remaining light on your feet (think about making as little noise on the track as you can).
2 Focus on the first part, the hop, as your foot will only move about 30–40 centimetres initially.
3 It is also possible to use this skipping drill as a strength exercise, aiming as far and as high as possible on each stride.

4 Drive the knee up and ensure that you are still 'running tall' and remaining in control.

Lunges

Lunges improve mobility and strength.

1 Take large steps, aiming to lunge a good distance.
2 Lower your hips towards the floor (the back leg knee shouldn't touch the floor).

This stretches the quadriceps, hip flexor, gluteal muscles (backside) and hamstrings, and also strengthens these areas when pulling up again to take the next lunge. Hold the position at the bottom of each step for a second or so.

General drills

Heel flicks

Working on this will ensure more rapid contact with the ground.

1 Run forwards taking short strides and flicking up with your feet to touch your backside with your heels (flick up as hard as possible but not moving forwards very far).
2 Make the flick-ups fast and as you progress in the drill, try to make the flick-ups progressively faster.
3 It is important to keep your upper leg, hip to knee, in line with the floor in this drill and you should try to have immediate lift off as soon as the foot touches the floor, also making as little noise as possible with each foot touch.

1, 2, flick

This is a progression from the heel-flick drill that requires a little more coordination.

1 Run with a very short, fast stride with feet coming up just a little behind, and then do an alternate flick-up every three strides to touch your backside as before.
2 You must ensure that you mentally focus on coordination, use the arms like pistons, and again, don't try to move forward too fast.

High knees

This is a drill that is used by many runners and triathletes, often without realizing why. The high knee drill is used for two reasons. Of course, it is used to learn to lift our knees up when running. This will help to maintain stride length rather than reducing it. But it is also to remind ourselves to be as light on our feet as possible, as this will reduce the amount of time spent in contact with the track (also a benefit of the two heel-flick drills above). Time spent in contact with the ground is energy absorbing and we should work on this during drills practice.

1 The drill is performed by lifting the knees high and bouncing or bounding with each stride and foot contact.

2 When working on this drill there can be a tendency to lean back as the knees come up – overcome this by running tall and looking forward rather than down at the knees.

3 The high knee drill can be worked at fairly slowly to begin with, gradually increasing the speed and intensity of the drill using the arms.

Rapid foot movement

If the single most important thing for fast running is a fast cadence, then this drill is essential.

1 Take very short steps, as little as 20-centimetres long, with the toes barely coming off the ground.

2 This stutter type action is done as fast as possible, almost a machine-gun type speed.

3 After around 20–30 of these machine-gun steps, open up the stride and run out. It is important to run tall, to lift the feet only a little, and to make little or no noise.

Kick through

This drill is particularly good for flexibility, control and coordination.

1 Take the first step on the right leg, the second step on the left leg, then kick a straight right leg up to the opposite (left) hand.

2 The support leg is on the ground but lifted onto the toes for a greater range of mobility.

3 This drill is best practised by walking through to begin with in order to get the coordination right before attempting to run through. Again, it is important to emphasize 'light feet'.

High knee lift, extend and drop

It is important not to confuse this drill with the 'high knees' drill as above.

1 Lift the knee, extend the leg forwards, drop the foot back to the ground just in front of the other foot.
2 Then bring in arms by raising the opposite arm as the knee is first lifted.

Sideways crossover forward and back

This drill can seem easy – it is basically running sideways with the legs crossing in front and behind each other as the athlete moves down the track, but some athletes have problems combining the front and rear crossover. It is worth walking through this drill first, then running, and finally bringing in the arms to counterbalance. When this is all mastered, use this drill initially then turn and run forwards.

Drill progression

All of these drills can be extended by combining them in running sessions: fast feet straight into high knees; straight into heel flicks; and so on. In practical terms, you would not just work on these running drills and nothing else. However, focusing on them during warm-ups and gradually building up the distance and number of drills will improve your running technique and ensure that there is little energy wasted when running hard in quality sessions.

Top tip

Occasionally it is valuable to use an entire running session to focus on these drills and run as many as five repetitions on four or five different drills up to a distance of 50 metres each. An extension of this is to drill run for 50 metres and move directly into full running for a further 50 metres but with emphasis on each particular aspect. This can add up to a fatiguing session incorporating both drills and hard, quality effort.

Speed and strength drills

The next set of drills focus on strength and speed: they are about elasticity, speed of contact with the ground and cadence. All these drills are about increasing speed by shortening the duration of the foot strike. Caution is required as they are very fatiguing and demanding. Do not attempt too many initially, particularly if you are just starting a running training programme, and make sure you are well warmed up before you begin any drills, particularly these as injury is possible if these are not performed properly.

High knee explosions, double foot jump

1 Stand tall but relaxed.
2 Begin by jumping very lightly on the spot, but then, while trying to hold the upright posture, do ten double foot jumps vertically while bringing both knees up towards your chest (use your arms to swing and balance).
3 Jump lightly for a few moments then repeat nine more times.
4 For beginners, five sets of ten repetitions is more than enough.

High knee explosions, single foot jump

As above but working on single leg (use opposite arm for balance). Jump lightly on both feet between repetitions. Note that this is a very demanding exercise.

One leg hops on the spot

1 Stand in a relaxed position, with your full body weight supported on your left foot only.
2 Lift your left heel slightly, so that the force of your body weight is passing through the ball of the left foot (your right knee is flexed so that your right foot is off the ground).
3 Then, hop on your left foot as fast as you can, aiming for three hops per second while trying to maintain a relaxed, upright posture.
4 The left foot should strike the ground in the area of the mid-foot and spring upwards rapidly, as though it has touched something very hot.
5 The hips should remain fairly level as you do this.

Alternate three hops

1 Start with three hops on the right foot, then three hops on your left, three more on your right, then left and keep repeating.
2 Begin with a total distance covered of 20 metres and gradually increase.
3 Hop with very springy, short steps, landing on the mid-foot area with each contact and springing upwards and forwards

after impact. Treat your ankles like coiled springs, compressing slightly with each mid-foot landing and then recoiling quickly.

4 Increase gradually up to six hops on each leg.

Indian hopping

1 Jog for a few strides, then hop diagonally forward and right on your right foot.

2 Immediately hop forward on the right foot, then hop diagonally to the left to land on your left foot.

3 Immediately hop forward to your left foot again, then hop diagonally forward onto your right foot.

4 Then hop forward to land again on your right; then hop diagonally to the left to land on your left foot; immediately hop forward to your left foot again.

5 Repeat for 20 metres and gradually build up to 40 metres.

Skip, run, 1-2-3

1 Begin with a high knee skip, so that your right thigh comes up to a position parallel with the ground as you skip (with two quick steps) on your left foot.

2 As soon as your right foot comes down, break into a very quick three-step (right, left, right) in which the last right step becomes the first step of the new skip.

3 As you skip on your right foot, bring your left thigh quickly up as before; as your left foot comes down, break into another three-step; left, right, left, with the third step initiating a new skip.

Chester/Scooter bounding

This is a very difficult drill both for strength and coordination. One leg is inactive, as though its foot is planted on the platform of a scooter. This foot only provides support while the bounding foot works explosively. With Chester bounding, you are learning to bound with one leg at a time.

1 Run along at a comfortable pace, but suddenly begin to make each foot strike with your right foot as explosive as possible.

2 As your right foot hits the ground, exert extra force with your right leg and foot while minimizing the time your right foot is in contact with the ground.

3 As you land on your left foot, simply make contact with the ground and then push off without any great force.

4 When the right foot hits the ground again, again aim for maximal force in the shortest possible time.

5 Repeat the pattern with the left foot making maximum force and the right leg acting as if riding on a scooter.

Imagine that you have a good (explosive) leg and a weak leg, and you are trying to generate the forward momentum from the good leg only.

Ladder running

A very useful piece of equipment is a running ladder. Basically, this is a rope ladder that is unfolded on the floor for athletes.

Drills used here are sequential, and they progress as follows:

1 Placing one foot in each square along the ladder.
2 Then speeding the foot plant up.
3 Then hopping.
4 Then double foot jumping.
5 Repeating all the above but using every other square.
6 Running and hopping in alternate squares.
7 Double foot jumping in and out of the square.
8 Double foot jumping on either side of the square, landing on the ball of the foot each time.

Training for triathlon running

As discussed in Chapter 03 on general principles of training, we know that the different types of training are:

1 long (endurance)
2 race pace (tempo)
3 and 4, interval and repetition training broken down into long and short distances, long and short recoveries
5 power and strength (hills, resistance)
6 quality
7 technique
8 mental toughness.

Technique for running has been discussed at length in this chapter, and later on Chapter 09 will cover mental toughness, therefore we have six remaining types of running training.

A good running training programme will cover all these aspects of training and the appropriate time of year to use each type. The difference between triathlon running and 'pure' running is that triathlon takes into the final discipline all the fatigue of having swam and cycled previously. This effect must be dealt with specifically and the efficiency of a good running technique and experience of having run after cycling (see Chapter 08 which covers back-to-back training) will make an enormous difference.

We must also consider that the time we have for triathlon running training is likely to be around one-third of that available for just running training. However, the plus side of running training is that it can be done anywhere, on any surface and at any time. Running is far easier to fit into a normal day than either swimming or cycling. Indeed, many runners within reasonable commuting distance will use their journey to and from work as their time for running training. However, if you do not come from a running background or have been away from running for some time, you must take care and not try to do too much too soon. The jarring effect of the impact of running can easily cause soreness and injury.

Training styles

Golden rules

1 In the very early stages, start slowly! Focus on covering the distance and gradually increase the amount of time that is spent running before attempting any type of interval, speed or quality training.
2 Always have a rest day between running days when starting out training, and run no more than three times each week (you might choose Monday, Wednesday and Friday) as you start to build up. Run for time rather than distance until you are comfortable with 30 minutes of non-stop running.
3 Make a rule for yourself of not attempting more than a 15 per cent increase in any six-week period. A cumulative 15 per cent increase every six weeks will mean that the training workload will increase by 70 per cent in a six-month period. In practical terms, an athlete initially running for 90 minutes each week will be running for two and a half hours each week after six months.

In the very early stages of training, there is nothing wrong with alternating running with walking until you become fitter. Let's look at a training programme for 'new' runners.

Running programme for new runners

Weeks 1 and 2	3 runs (or run/walks) × 20 minutes each
Weeks 3 and 4	2 runs × 20 minutes, 1 run × 25 minutes
Weeks 5 and 6	1 run × 20 minutes, 2 runs × 25 minutes

This initial six-week period gives an increase of ten minutes from 60 to 70 minutes, just over a 15 per cent increase in running time.

Weeks 7 and 8	1 run × 20 minutes, 1 run × 25 minutes, 1 run × 30 minutes
Weeks 9 and 10	2 runs × 25 minutes, 1 run × 30 minutes
Weeks 11 and 12	2 runs only × 30 minutes with extra rest day
Weeks 13 and 14	1 run × 25 minutes, 1 run × 30 minutes, 1 run × 35 minutes
Weeks 15 and 16	2 runs × 30 minutes, 1 run × 40 minutes
Weeks 17 and 18	2 runs × 30 minutes, 1 run × 45 minutes

By following this programme, in a relatively short time period of just over four months, you will have achieved the following:

- increased your running time by 45 minutes each week
- have one run each week more than double the time of the first week.

You should now be ready to introduce some variety into your running training programme.

Fartlek

Fartlek is a Swedish word meaning 'speed-play'. It is a good method of introducing some quality into running training without too much pressure. You simply increase your speed and pace when you want to during your run, for as long or as short a period of time as you are able. Fartlek will teach you about your body and its reaction to training; seeing and feeling a sudden increase in heart rate when attempting to speed up for the first time, and its subsequent drop when speed eases off, gives a practical oversight of the body's reaction to the stress of training hard.

Using fartlek as the first introduction to speed work where the ratio of hard to easy efforts is at your discretion ensures that you will not become over-fatigued. If you choose to remain at the time content of the final two weeks introduction to running (weeks 17 and 18 above) and introduce fartlek into just one of the runs, a gradual overload and progression is assured, and you can monitor the increase in training load. The next progression might be to increase the periods of fast running.

How to increase the fast running sections in fartlek

WEEK 1	Include in the 30 minute run: 5 efforts of 30 seconds with a 60 second interval recovery jog
WEEK 2	Include in the 30 minute run: 5 efforts of 30 seconds with a 60 second interval recovery jog
WEEK 3	Include in the 30 minute run: 6 efforts of 40 seconds with a 50 second interval recovery jog
WEEK 4	Include in the 30 minute run: 8 efforts of 40 seconds with a 50 second interval recovery jog
WEEK 5	Include in the 30 minute run: 8 efforts of 40 seconds with a 40 second interval recovery jog
WEEK 6	Include in the 30 minute run: 4 efforts of 60 seconds with a 45 second interval recovery jog

During these six weeks, even with only slight increases there is a substantial increase in workload over the time period.

Interval and repetition training

After the initial introduction to fartlek and a realization of how effort will affect your body, you are ready to move on to structured interval training. Contrary to popular belief, **interval** refers to the resting interval between efforts, rather than the effort.

The terms interval training and repetition training have become almost synonymous, however **interval training** usually has a fairly short rest between a large number of efforts whereas **repetition training** will have a considerably longer recovery but will focus on quality. If you have followed the fartlek outline programme above, your **interval** training session might look like this:

- 12 × 200 metres working at 80 per cent of maximum effort with 100 metres jog recovery (30 seconds)

or, for a **repetition** training session, you might do:

- 4 × 200 metres working at 95 per cent of maximum effort with three minutes walking recovery.

The repetition session efforts will be run faster than the interval session efforts. The amount of work done in the interval session is greater, but the quality of work in the repetition is much higher.

When you have accepted interval-type workouts as part of your running training, it is important that the training becomes both varied and progressive. As you become more experienced, your interval session in each of six weeks might look similar to that below.

Progressive interval training programme

WEEK 1	Warm-up 15 × 30 seconds stride effort 30 seconds easy jog recovery (as session above)
WEEK 2	Warm-up 4 × 2 minutes at 85 per cent effort 60 seconds easy jog recovery
WEEK 3	Warm-up 10 × 1 min at 90 per cent effort 60 seconds easy jog recovery

WEEK 4	Warm-up 4 × 3 minutes at 85 per cent effort 60 seconds easy jog recovery
WEEK 5	Warm-up 3 × 6 minutes at just faster than estimated ten kilometre racing pace effort 2 minutes easy jog recovery
WEEK 6	Warm-up 7 × 3 minutes at just faster than estimated ten kilometre racing pace effort 2 minutes easy jog recovery

This six-week phase of training fits our criteria for variety and progression. The timing of the efforts vary between 30 seconds and six minutes; the recovery times between 30 seconds and two minutes; and the amount of hard work in each session progresses from 7.5 minutes in week 1, up to 21 minutes in week 6.

Hill training

It might seem strange, but many runners have weak legs. If you don't incorporate technique and quality training sessions into your schedule, you will become used to running or jogging at relatively slow speeds and therefore won't possess the spring and cadence that is necessary for faster running. Hill running is an excellent way of building strength in legs (and particularly useful in the run if your triathlon is uphill!).

* Include hilly runs in your steady and endurance sessions.
* Run progressively faster up the hill.
* Join together hill and interval training by running up an incline, jogging down, and then repeating a number of times. You might run six repetitions up a hill that takes 30 seconds, and allow 60 seconds for the jog down recovery.

Race pace (tempo)

It is important that you run some of your training sessions at race pace. These sessions are extremely hard and demanding, so the total time of effort at racing pace should normally be less than the estimated racing time. For example, if you are hoping to run 25 minutes for the five kilometres of a sprint triathlon, you would run for perhaps 15 minutes for your tempo training session. As necessarily demanding as training sessions must be, it is essential that they are not always flat-out. The euphoria and excitement of a race will bring about that extra effort and speed for an increased time.

Running training schedules

Set out below are two examples of six-week training plans during different times of the year. The first example is that of a new triathlete who had been a runner, beginning training in winter. Each week features three different runs.

WEEK 1	40 minute steady run Hilly run, 40 minutes Long, easy run, 60 minutes
WEEK 2	40 minute steady run Hilly run 50 minutes Long, easy run, 60–70 minutes
WEEK 3	40 minute steady run Long, easy run, 60–70 minutes Hill run – warm-up, then 12 × 90 seconds with jog-down recovery (1 hour including warm-up)
WEEK 4	Hilly run, 60 minutes Hills as in week 3 40 minute run – 5 minutes easy, then 30 minutes of interval running (30 seconds steady/fast and 30 seconds striding in between) Easy 5 minute run to finish
WEEK 5	Hilly run, 60 minutes Hills as in week 4 but increase running sections to 45 seconds and reduce striding to 15 seconds Long, easy run for 80 minutes
WEEK 6	Hilly run, 60 minutes Hill run as week 5 but increase time by 10 minutes Long run, 80 minutes, very easy and relaxed

This second example is of the same triathlete one year on, with three runs per week. This training schedule was just before the summer, the pre-competitive period.

WEEK 1	30 minute run with very hard pace 2 × 6 minutes (recovery 1 minute jog) Steady 40 minute run with 10 × 40 seconds fast stride, 40 seconds jog recovery 40 minute run to include hills with a maximum of 10 minutes running uphill
WEEK 2	10 kilometre acceleration session Reducing recovery 200 metres session (see below) Steady 40 minute run
WEEK 3	4 × 1500 metre at race pace with 1 minute recovery only Steady 40 minutes with two sets of 10 × 30 seconds fast strides, 30 seconds jog recovery, 3 minutes easy run between the two sets Steady 40 minute run
WEEK 4	Hilly 10 kilometre acceleration session*, 60 minutes Reducing recovery 200 metres session* Steady 40 minutes
WEEK 5	40 minute run with very hard pace 8 × 3 minutes (recovery 1 minute only jog). This session should be run at race pace. Reducing recovery 200 metres* 40 minute run to include hills with a maximum of 10 minutes running uphill
WEEK 6 RECOVERY WEEK	30 minute interval run Very hard race pace 7 minutes, recovery 1 minute jog × 3 Second run, reduce recovery to 200 metres

*See overleaf

There is an immediate contrast between the two training schedules which reflects the difference after a year's experience and the different times of the year. These specific training sessions are explained here.

Reducing recovery 200 metres session

It is important that you have a reasonable idea of your projected running speed for this session. I have based the pace for this example on an athlete who would run between 48 to 50 minutes for a ten kilometre race. This is approximately an eight-minute mile pace which works out to 200 metres per minute. We take off ten seconds, so the aim is to run at 50 seconds for each 200 metre repetition, significantly faster than race pace. If you are unable to measure the exact distance you are running, simply run for 50 seconds.

This is what a Reducing Recovery 200 metres session looks like. After your normal running warm-up:

1 Run the first 200 metres in 50 seconds, it should feel like a hard effort but by no means flat-out.
2 After this first 200-metre run, jog for 90 seconds.
3 Repeat the 200-metre run; then jog for 75 seconds.
4 Repeat the 200 metres again, this time jog for 60 seconds.
5 Run 200 metres, jog for 45 seconds.
6 Run 200 metres, jog for 30 seconds.
7 Run 200 metres, jog for 15 seconds.
8 Run 200 metres.

After this 200-metre effort, revert to a jog for 90 seconds and repeat the reducing recovery cycle again. If you are still maintaining your speed, pace and running technique, repeat it three times in total.

The first set gives you 7×200 metre repetitions; then a further set gives you 6×200 metres each time; going through the full set three times makes 19 repetitions. It teaches you to maintain a fast speed when you are getting progressively tired, and goes a long way to simulating race conditions. If you feel able to go through for a fourth series of efforts, it is likely that the running speed of each repetition has not been set fast enough. Equally, if you are not able to maintain the projected speed through the first set of seven repetitions, then the likelihood is that the pace aimed for is too ambitious.

Ten kilometre pace acceleration session

This is for maintaining and increasing run speed when you are tired or under pressure. For this session you aim to run progressively faster as you become more fatigued. The essential thing is that the recovery phases are carefully controlled – it is more a backing off of pace than a recovery phase, as the 'recovery' phase is a run at around a ten kilometre racing pace.

In this example, the times are based on a runner capable of running ten kilometres in 39 to 40 minutes, which equates to approximately 18.45 for 5000 metres.

This is what a ten kilometre pace acceleration session looks like. After your normal running warm-up:

1 Run 400 metres at three seconds faster than your five kilometre racing pace; so this 400 metres is aimed at 87 seconds in this example.
2 Have 400 metres recovery at ten kilometre race pace (for this athlete about one minute 40 seconds – remember, all the recovery phases are done at this pace, this is important).
3 300 metres at 3000 metres pace (60–3 seconds).
4 300 metres recovery in about 75 seconds (ten kilometre race pace).
5 200 metres at 1500 metre pace, (approximately one to two seconds faster at 200 metres than the 300 metre repetition pace, so 37–40 seconds).
6 200 metres recovery in about 50 seconds (ten kilometre race pace).
7 100 metres at near sprint (800 metre pace) but staying in control of technique and form.
8 100 metres recovery in 25 seconds (ten kilometre race pace).

This is a tough session! However, as you become more experienced it is possible to go through the above session once, or even twice more. However, this demanding session, going through the three sets of these repetitions, gives 6000 metres, and for most of us, this is enough.

However as you get fitter you might try a couple of minutes of easy jogging, and then repeat the above, but this time going through the sets twice only rather than three times, five times in all. And if you get really fit, go through one more time. If you manage to work up to the extra sets, that extra 4000 metres makes 10,000 in all; if you hang in for all six sets, you've done 12,000 metres of which 6000 metres is extremely demanding – faster than race pace for an Olympic distance event – and 6000 metres is at that race pace!

So, if you have worked through the running drills in this section, you should have seen your running technique and style improve, and along with that, your running pace increase. One of the most difficult things about running in a triathlon is that it is the final event to be completed, but if you follow the tips throughout this book – helping you to save muscular energy being spent in the legs during the swim and cycle – you now only need to master the cycle-run transition to get you settled into your run. So let's take a look at that fourth discipline now – the transition.

08 transition and back-to-back training

In this chapter you will learn:
- what a transition area is
- how to plan your transition
- the secrets of a super-fast transition
- about back-to-back training.

The changeover from swimming to cycling and then from cycling to running in triathlon is called the transition: it is known as the fourth discipline. This combination of the three individual disciplines of swimming, cycling and running is what makes triathlon what it is, a unique sport.

Throughout this chapter you will pick up tips that will knock valuable time off your triathlon race time. From using Vaseline to enable a quicker wetsuit exit, leaving a brightly coloured balloon floating above your bike, to fixing cycling shoes in the pedals, you are guaranteed to become familiar with the tricks of the trade that seasoned triathletes use.

The transition area

The area in race events where the transition takes place is called the transition area. Nobody apart from athletes and race marshalls are allowed into the transition area. The two transitions are sometimes known as T1 (swim to bike) and T2 (bike to run). The transition area is where clothing and shoes are taken off and put on, and where the necessary equipment for the next part of the race is located. If you are just beginning to take part in triathlons, it is worthwhile practising changing clothes and shoes from the swim to cycle phase, and the cycle to run phase at home, as this will speed up your transitions on race day.

Planning your transition

As there is a 'running clock' in triathlon events, it is essential that athletes are smooth and fast in transition. Working on the transition phase is an essential part of triathlon training and can easily make a significant difference in the overall finishing time of a race. It is very easy for the newcomer to panic in the transition phase and actually lose time: there seems to be so much to think about, so many different things to do: crash helmet, shoes, vest or top, number fixed correctly, sunglasses... Not only is it the number of things to do, crucially it is the order of doing them.

There are many triathletes out there who will have memories of putting on their crash helmet for the bike section and then realizing that they can't get their cycle top over their head because of this. The secret is to be orderly and have good planning; this does not mean slow. Experienced athletes will have a mental checklist in their heads, an order of what to do and when to do it.

Top tip

A recommendation for new triathletes is to write down what you have to do and the order you need to do them in – a to-do list. Think through and learn this order so that it becomes an automatic response in the transition area. As with all skills, they look so easy when executed by a top athlete and so difficult by a novice. It is not unusual to see a top triathlete taking less than ten seconds to change from cycling to running mode, including racking the bike, taking off the crash helmet and cycle shoes, and putting on running shoes and any other necessary clothing. Equally, it is not unusual to see a new triathlete taking a minute or even two minutes to do these things.

When you're in transition the most essential aspect is to be quick, but not so quick that you become disorientated. If you haven't practised before and you rush, things will go wrong and you will end up wasting time rather than saving it. The old maxim of 'more haste, less speed' becomes true without the necessary practice before the race.

What to wear

The choice of what kit to wear is entirely up to the individual. Most experienced triathletes will choose to go through the entire race in whatever they do the swim in, either a swimming costume or a tri-suit. Men will need to put on a top, while women will, of course, already have their tops covered. However, there is complete freedom to change between disciplines and you may choose to change out of a costume into cycling shorts and top, and then into running shorts and vest. Of course, changing clothes between disciplines will take a lot more time. Nudity is not allowed in transition, so if you are going to change, make sure you have a towel with you. Wearing socks, particularly for the run, will be more comfortable if you have never run without socks before, but putting socks on over wet feet can be very time-consuming.

Usually the transition area is the same one for swim to cycle and for cycle to run. However, occasionally, because of the logistics of the particular event there can be two separate and different transition areas. These can be several miles apart and will mean that you have to take all your running kit and equipment to a different transition area and familiarize yourself with it – before returning to the swim venue to begin the race. It is important to read all the race information when entering a new event to ensure that you don't have any nasty surprises on the day.

Speed through transition

Large events will have a different entrance and exit for both transitions to ensure that athletes don't get in each others' way. It is important that you locate the entrances and exits and then walk through this when setting up your kit and equipment. A very general rule of thumb might be that the entrance to transition from the swim will be at a different end of the transition area to the exit on the bike, and that the entrance from the bike will be different to the exit on the run. For smaller events with only a few athletes, this may not be necessary and the onus will be on the athletes to avoid each other.

Frequently there will be a 'one-way system' operating when there are different ins and outs to transition. Make sure that you know the direction of flow through the transition area. It might appear that this is 'information overkill' and a lot to take in before a race, but it is better to be over-prepared than not. You will also usually find that the entrance and exit routes are well marked, and race marshals will guide you through the transition area where necessary.

Swim-to-bike transition (T1)

Many new triathletes choose to enter an event where the swim discipline is in a swimming pool. For the transition this could easily mean running through a changing room, along a corridor and even up or down stairs before getting into the transition area and onto your bike. Open water events will not require this, although some longer triathlons where the swim is in the sea will have a shower tent so that athletes can wash off the salt from their bodies.

Whether the swim is indoors or outdoors, you must know the route to take to get to your bike. You will have your goggles, swim hat and wetsuit (if worn) to take off and there may often be rules as to where to put them. Certainly, you will not want to lose your wetsuit or goggles by just throwing them away as you run in from the swim.

Top tip

Take a buddy! Although non-competitors are not allowed in the transition area, there may be somewhere that a friend/partner/coach can stand whilst you swim. You can leave your goggles and swim hat (and wetsuit) with them without having to worry about picking them up later.

Also having a friend on the sidelines may mean that you can leave your cycling kit laid out ready to jump in to, without having anyone inadvertently move it.

Sequence of transition: T1

1 As you are running from the swim finish towards the transition, undo the zip of the wetsuit halfway down.
2 Have your goggles away from your eyes on your forehead.
3 As you approach your bike, pull down the wetsuit zip completely.
4 Left hand goes onto right shoulder, grip the wetsuit and pull down over the arm and hand.
5 Repeat this with the right hand pulling down the left arm of the wetsuit.
6 Place both hands on the wetsuit and pull down over the hips.
7 Keep pulling down over the legs.
8 When the bulk of the wetsuit is on the ground, use each foot to stand on the other leg of the wetsuit to get the lower leg, heel and foot out.
9 Take goggles and swim hat off and place by your transition zone.
10 Put your cycle top on.
11 Make sure your number is on (either pinned onto the vest or attached with elastic).
12 Put on cycle shorts (if intending to wear them).
13 Put on cycle shoes or trainers (and socks if required).

14 Put on crash helmet.
15 Put on shades (sunglasses) if wearing them.
16 Unrack your bike and run with it out of the transition towards the mount line.

On and off the bike

In the large, popular events there may be several thousand competitors racing. Race organizers will often create a 'novice' start in a large event and this is an excellent way to get a real flavour of what triathlon is all about, as well as having the safety of being in the swim section with other first-timers. The athletes are started in 'wave' starts on the swim to ensure safety. Even so, there can be over 100 competitors in any one wave-start, which means that there can be a lot of athletes coming out of the swim and into transition very close together. This can feel both claustrophobic and disorientating, particularly as your heart will be beating fast, you may well have water in your eyes and you will be thinking of getting out of that wetsuit as quickly as you can. Then, as you enter transition, you are confronted by rows and rows of racked bikes. What looked simple and clear when you walked through by yourself can be very different in the heat of competition.

In most triathlons now, the bikes are put on scaffolding type racks in the transition area and competitors will have their race number pasted onto the rack to show where to rack the bikes. Bikes can be racked by either placing the underside of the saddle or the handlebars on the metal bar. It is worthwhile deciding and practising exactly how you will rack your bike by racking and unracking several times and choosing which is best for you.

Top tip

Don't forget to leave a filled water bottle with your bike – it's likely you'll want a drink after the swim (particularly if you've swallowed any salty or chlorinated water), and the cycle part of the race is the easiest section to re-hydrate if you have a bottle mount on your bike.

If there are a lot of different rows of bikes, make sure that when you go through transition before the race, you count how many rows there are when you enter transition from swim or bike.

Top tip

Be tactical! You need to ensure that you can find your bike (amongst hundreds of others) quickly. Although some race organizers will not allow any distinctive marks to be made in transition area, many will do so, and a brightly-coloured crash helmet, towel or water bottle can be extremely useful in finding your place in the transition area when you're running in hard to save time. Some athletes will have small balloons or something distinctive placed high up over their position so that they can easily see it as they come running in.

The next essential is locating exactly where the 'mount' line is. For safety reasons, no cycling is allowed in the transition area as it is a restricted area filled with competitors. There will usually be a line painted on the road just outside transition where you are allowed to mount your bike. You will need to walk or run with your bike to the cycle exit of transition. It is important that you have your crash helmet clipped tightly on your head before you take your bike from the racking – crash helmets must be secure and no elastic or 'loose' tie ups are permitted.

Bike-to-run transition (T2)

At the end of the bike section as you approach the cycle entrance into transition, you are likely to be greeted by marshals blowing whistles. This is to remind you that, as with the mount line going out on the bike, there is a dismount line before entering transition. Again, it is essential that you know where to dismount, as infringement of this rule will lead to a time penalty. After dismounting, you must place or rack your bike, and only then can you unclip and take off your crash helmet. We then repeat a similar procedure to T1 by putting on running shoes and getting to the run exit.

For both transitions, when setting up your own transition space with your kit and equipment, ensure that it's set out logically so you can easily reach and put on the clothing that you need first.

> **Top tip**
>
> If you're going to wear a vest or T-shirt, have your racing numbers pinned on already – make sure that you don't pin the number through both front and back of the vest!
>
> If the race organizer allows you to use elastic to attach the numbers on, it might be worth considering wearing the number underneath your wetsuit.

Sequence of transition: T2

As you approach the end of bike discipline:

1 Undo your cycle shoes from pedals or undo cycle shoelaces/velcro and put feet on top of shoes while leaving them attached to pedals.
2 Dismount bike by line.
3 Run with and push your bike to your own space.
4 Rack bike.
5 Unfasten and take off your bike helmet.
6 Take off your shoes if not already done.
7 Change shorts (if changing kit).
8 Sunglasses on/off?
9 Put on running shoes (unless you cycled in running shoes).
10 Run out of transition.

Secrets of a super-fast transition

The fewer changes of clothes that you make the more time you will save.

Wear less, don't change! The minimum that you need to wear is either a tri-suit or a swimming costume (women) or swimming shorts (men) – men will need to put on a vest or top as well for the cycle and run if wearing shorts.   .

- If the swim requires a wetsuit, then women can have the number already pinned to the swimming costume or tucked down the back of the costume on elastic ready to pull on.
- A vest is better than a T-shirt as T-shirt sleeves can slow down putting it on, especially as the upper body will be wet from the swim and may lead to the top sticking to the moist skin surface.

- Dry-fit, polyester-type fabrics are easier to slip over wet bodies than cotton (and also much better to race in).
- Men should lay out the vest with it folded from the bottom up so that only a little more than the openings for head and arms are visible. This lessens any chance of the vest getting caught or sticking.
- Numbers should already be attached. Use four pins, one at each corner to lessen any possibility of the number sticking, scratching or getting torn and then flapping about during the cycle section.
- Have your crash helmet positioned upside down on your handlebars with the front of the crash helmet towards you. In this way it can simply be lifted with one hand on each side and placed on your head.
- If you are intending to wear sunglasses or clear glasses (they can help avoid getting grit or dirt in the eyes), place them opened inside the crash helmet. Do be aware that shades or glasses will easily mist up as sweating will create heat and you may need to wipe them clean at the start of the cycle. If you do wipe them, ensure that your hands don't have any grease on them from taking off your wetsuit; grease on glasses is not a good idea!
- Tying up laces is time-consuming. It is best to invest in lacelocks (see Chapter 02) or use elastic laces so that the shoes can be pulled on with no time-wasting tying up.
- Some triathletes will choose to do the cycle section in running shoes, particularly when the race is extremely short (supersprint) or if it is a duathlon (run–bike–run). Thompson pedal adaptors will make the ride more efficient if this option is chosen.

Wetsuit tips

Although it is a personal choice, some wetsuits now have the back zip opening from the bottom rather than the top, which does make it a little easier to locate the cord and pull up rather than down.

- Have the cord/velcro end down where it is easily accessible to grab hold of.
- Moisten the very bottom of the legs of the wetsuits with a little Vaseline; this will allow the wetsuit to slip over the heels more easily.

- Similarly, cycle and running shoes can have either a little Vaseline at the heels or some talcum powder sprinkled inside to facilitate entry.

Cycle shoe tips

As you become more experienced, you can experiment in training with having your cycle shoes already clipped into the cycle pedals. This is a difficult skill initially as it means having to place your feet in the shoes as you are already riding, but it does become much easier with practice and can save a lot of time. Also practise mounting your bike as you are running alongside it, rather than stopping and mounting from a standstill, as this will save considerable time. It is worth training on soft ground, perhaps grass, to start with as you may well fall over in the beginning stages.

There are a number of things you can do to make these two skills easier; have the pedals and cranks positioned parallel to the ground in a flat position by using Blu-tack and a matchstick to hold their position. Similarly, an elastic band around the back of the shoe and the crank will hold that horizontal position as well, and make getting the feet into the shoes relatively simple.

Top tip

Although transitions may sound complicated, it is an integral and essential part of triathlon and once done, the process becomes clear. Have a plan and a mental picture of what to do and where everything is, and above all, go through transition before the race starts. As with the training disciplines of swimming, cycling and running, practice makes perfect, and the transition is no exception. So create your own transition areas at home, lay out your kit, and practise changing from one discipline to the other.

The muscular transition between disciplines

The transition between disciplines also creates a transition between which muscles are being exercised, and this changeover needs practising just as much as the practical elements of each transition.

What to expect

Be aware that swimming is mainly an upper body activity and blood will be pooled there rather than in the legs. In the early stages of the bike section the blood will need to relocate to the legs; the feeling of emptiness in the legs is a symptom of this and will quickly go away.

The change from cycling to running can be much more traumatic for the legs; they will already be tired from cycling and there is a significant difference between the circular motions on the bike with very little or no impact, and the up and down running motion with impact and pounding as the feet hit the ground. Some triathletes liken the feeling in the bottom of the feet to having a block of wood inside the shoe. It is better to take short, fast strides initially as you begin running; over-striding will have a braking effect and slow you down.

However, the good news is that these feelings can be overcome to an extent with something called back-to-back or brick training. This is essentially just practising the changeover from swim to cycle, and cycle to run.

Back-to-back and brick training

Training in one discipline followed immediately by training in another discipline is called back-to-back training. Training across the disciplines continuously is called brick training. In triathlon, swimming followed by cycling or cycling followed by running is back-to-back training while cycle to run to cycle to run (more than just going through the cycle to run sequence just once) is a brick session.

The best way to excel in sport is to ensure that much of your training is similar to the event you plan to compete in, which makes swimming then cycling, and cycling then running essential training for triathlon. Back-to-back training and brick training replicate the feeling of discomfort in racing and changing disciplines. They are extremely demanding sessions and, if you are new to triathlon, you should be cautious of attempting too much too soon; adequate rest and recovery is essential.

For some individuals these training sessions give immediate benefits, for others very little more is achieved than the gains made in individual training in swimming, cycling or running. The combination sessions must be specific to you as an individual. Some people find that they cannot cope at all with these sessions, whilst others make the transition with no problems. For endurance events i.e. longer triathlon races, you should plan longer swims followed by long cycle rides, or long cycle rides followed by longer runs, always mimicking the race distances you are training for.

Swim-to-cycle training sessions

This type of session prepares you for the feelings of discomfort during a race in the swim-to-cycle transition when the effort and muscular output is transferred from the upper body to the lower body.

For convenience, all or most cycling elements set out here can be done on the road or on a turbo trainer. Here are some example back-to-back training sessions:

- 400-metre swim followed immediately by a cycle for 30 minutes.
- *First progression:* 600-metre swim followed immediately by a cycle for 45 minutes.
- *Second progression:* 800-metre swim followed immediately by a cycle for one hour.
- *Third progression:* 1500-metre swim followed immediately by a cycle for 90 minutes.

Swim-to-cycle transition

We looked at the swim to bike back-to-back session above but you may want to simulate more closely the swim to bike transition. Many athletes don't give any training time to the swim to bike changeover. The session outlined below may create logistical difficulties as it needs you to set up a turbo trainer by a swimming pool, but most swimming pools do have a club room, gym or training space where a turbo bike can be set up, and this brick training session (or variations on it) will help with your swim-to-bike transitions.

- Warm-up in the swimming pool as you would for a race.
- Do a 400-metre swim at race pace followed by eight minutes cycling on the turbo trainer at race pace or slightly faster.
- Repeat this up to five times depending on fitness levels.

Another option is to reduce the swim distance from 400 metres to 300 metres. Take a couple of minutes after each turbo set to stretch out, or you'll be going into the next swim with blood pooling in the legs and you won't get the most out of the session. This swim-to-bike training session gives not only the chance to simulate the feeling of getting onto the bike after a hard swim, but also to go through the mechanics of transition and putting on shoes and necessary clothes.

Cycle-to-run training sessions

This is more demanding than the swim to cycle sessions. The legs are already fatigued from cycling and then have to run. There is also the added dimension of the circular effort of cycling being replaced by the up and down motion of running. Initially, it is very uncomfortable but the discomfort does ease with adequate training. The ability to run well during a triathlon event is as much to do with coping with the transition effect as being a strong runner. Here are some example back-to-back training sessions:

- Cycle for 30 minutes followed immediately by a run for 15 minutes.
- *First progression:* cycle for 45 minutes followed immediately by a run for 25 minutes.
- *Second progression:* cycle for 60 minutes followed immediately by a run for 35 minutes.
- *Third progression:* cycle for 90 minutes, followed immediately by a run for 45 minutes.

All these training sessions above are endurance based and progressive.

If you would like to progress towards a race, a little more race pace speed can be injected into some, but not all, of the sessions. These sessions will normally enter into the training schedule in pre-competition phase (just before the racing time of year). As you approach the racing season, it becomes even more important to try to simulate racing conditions so that your first race is not a huge shock to the system. As such, these sessions focus on achieving a specific running speed.

- Cycle steady but not hard for 30, 45 or 60 minutes followed by a 30 minute run. The run section includes 5 × 3 minutes aiming at the projected racing speed with just one minute easy jogging in between the three minute efforts.
- *First progression:* One hour cycle ride followed by 45 minute run.

The cycle is easy to begin with so gradually increase the effort and speed every ten minutes. Judge the increase either by putting up the speed by half a mile an hour each time, or another way of judging is to estimate your own perceived rate of exertion (RPE) on a scale of 1 to 20 and put the RPE up every ten minutes. The RPE is how hard you think that you are working. A turbo trainer is very useful for this type of session.

The run is as follows:

- ten minutes easy to steady
- 30 sets of 30 seconds effort (faster than race pace) with a 30 second jog recovery between each hard session.
- five minutes easy jog to cool-down.

- *Second progression*: 75 minute cycle, steady but not hard followed by a 45 minute run.

The run is as follows:

- seven minutes easy
- five minutes hard (at projected racing pace or faster) then two minutes easy
- five minutes hard (at racing pace or faster) then two minutes easy
- five minutes hard (at racing pace or faster) then two minutes easy
- five minutes hard (at racing pace or faster)
- twelve minutes cool-down.

You are beginning now to simulate the conditions and pain felt during a race, but still maintaining an endurance element (45 minute run). After this phase, you should start to focus much more specifically on speed.

Cycle-to-run transition

A fast brick session as shown below has proved to be very efficient in building speed and strength:

- Cycle for five kilometre or for ten minutes.
- Run for one kilometre or five minutes.
- Repeat five times in one session.

Again, it is best to do the cycle section on a turbo trainer here. Each cycle section should aim at slightly faster than your projected race pace, and each run done hard. You shouldn't take any recovery between each phase of cycling to running or from running to cycling.

The progression here becomes very race specific. The cycle section pace remains the same but each succeeding run phase is a little faster. Practically, this means that whatever time you do your first run in, each run after this one should be around ten seconds faster each time. This session not only gives you practice for the transition of cycling to running, but it also simulates the effort needed to maintain running pace during a race.

As with previous examples of training sessions, the amount of repetitions, speeds and times can all be adjusted to suit you and your current standard of fitness and experience. It is important to maintain good form and technique on the run when doing this session, and you should remember to try to maintain your run cadence at 180 foot strikes per minute if possible (see Chapter 07). This session teaches you to run faster as you become more fatigued from each preceding effort. It is a very demanding session but has great benefits.

It is important to emphasize again that brick training can be very physically and mentally demanding. Be cautious, and take advice from your coach and from more experienced athletes when embarking upon this type of training.

Top tip

So remember:

- Practise changing out of and into your chosen attire before race day.
- Use as many time-saving tips as you can!
- Read the triathlon briefing pack carefully.
- Visit the transition areas and familiarize yourself with them.
- Incorporate back-to-back and brick training into your training schedule.

09

mental attitude and confidence

In this chapter you will learn:
- what mental skills really are
- how to maintain motivation and concentration
- how to deal with anxiety and worry
- how to use relaxation and tension
- how to build confidence.

It's important to consider the psychological aspects of training and racing as well as the physiological elements we are all so familiar with. Mental attitude and mental toughness are skills: maintaining motivation when things sometimes become unpleasant (poor weather, feeling tired, or problems outside triathlon) can be difficult even if you want to train. There are a number of simple things that we can do to maintain motivation and to keep a positive mental attitude.

Maintaining motivation

Have you ever asked yourself the following questions in the midst of your triathlon training?

- Do I really want to do this?
- Am I being realistic?
- Do I have the time?
- Can I fit in this lifestyle with my normal work?
- Is it compatible with my family life?
- Can I physically accept the training required?
- Can I afford it?

All these thoughts are real, practical elements that can get in the way of training. Sometimes it's easy to forget exactly why you started, so why not write down a few of the reasons that you did start. Perhaps it was to lose weight, or to feel more alive, maybe you watched a triathlon race and were inspired. Sometimes it's important to write things down to make them more real.

Top tip

Did you know there are proven psychological benefits involved in racing and competitive sport? Perhaps it is this feeling of optimism, vitality and energy that made you start and makes you want to continue with your triathlon training?

Goal setting

Setting goals is an essential part of any serious training programme, and writing your goals down has been shown to increase the probability of achieving them. Set out your aims of what you intend to do this year: to swim 800 metres without stopping, to run five miles in the local fun run, to enter and finish your first race. Ideally, you should have some long-term and short-term goals. The long-term goals, maybe something you want to achieve in six months or a year's time, should be broken down into smaller steps to make them more achievable.

The SCAMP process

Coaches and psychologists often talk about the **SCAMP** process. This means making your goals and aims:

- **S**pecific
- **C**hallenging
- **A**ttainable
- **M**easurable
- **P**ersonal.

Thinking about and setting these SCAMP ideas will have a tremendous influence on how you go about your new involvement in triathlon. It may be a good idea to talk about your aims with someone who has been involved in triathlon a little longer than you, and use their experience.

When you achieve any of these goals that you've set yourself, you should reward yourself. It can be as simple as a bar of chocolate, but it can mean as much as a medal. Maybe you'll buy yourself a new piece of triathlon kit.

Staying focused and identifying barriers

After the initial excitement of starting on a new challenge, it can be easy to lose concentration and motivation after a few weeks (psychologists tell us it can take as much as six weeks to accept and keep to a new way of doing things). What can you do to keep this focus? Deciding what your likely distractions are, the things that will most put you off, is important. Again, writing these things down will make you think about them and make them real. With a list of your barriers to training, when these occur you will recognize them and be better prepared to deal with them, especially if you've thought of ways to get around each barrier beforehand.

Visualization

When you've thought about the 'bad' things, take a minute to see yourself in a good scene. Psychologists call this visualization.

Visualization exercise

Sit down quietly by yourself and close your eyes, then just picture yourself taking part and doing well in that first race that you've set yourself. It's important to see yourself from the outside, as if it's someone else competing. Make the picture in colour and focus on how good you look, how good you feel, and how pleased you are with yourself for putting in all the effort that has taken you to this event. If you can't imagine it, you can't do it!

This 'imagining' is a very powerful way of keeping concentration and motivation going, even when other factors outside your control may make it difficult. Whenever you have just a few minutes to yourself, use them to sit quietly and repeat the process of visualization.

Positive rationalization

Another athlete that I was privileged to work with was Andy Mouncey. Every triathlete has experienced that awful feeling during the latter stages of the bike or maybe the run when all the energy has seemingly drained out of the body and there is still a long, long way to go! When Andy reached the top of one particular mountain in a race in France a few years ago, he was so exhausted that he climbed off his bike and sat there with his head in his hands. It was over.

Except that, for him, it wasn't.

He rationalized exactly what he was doing, his mind thinking 'I knew I'd feel like this sometime, we anticipated it in training. But am I going to waste all that training that I've done to get here? I will feel better, I need to eat and drink, I need to focus on what I'm going to do right now and put this behind me. I knew this was going to happen and now it has. I know what to do, I can do it.'

He ate; he drank; he stretched. He climbed back on his bike after a break that was at most five minutes and focused completely on the next stage of the race, breaking up all those miles into single ones and mentally ticking them off as he went through that long day. And he finished – not only finished – but in a more than respectable time.

Combating anxiety and worry

As you get closer to your first race, it is likely that you will start to get anxious about it. This is completely normal. We will have a look at building confidence later in this chapter, and the anxiety or worrying that can occur is the other side of the coin to creating that confidence in yourself. There is nothing wrong in worrying, it's entirely natural, but it is important to recognize it for what it is and to find ways to overcome or reduce it.

Muscle tension and relaxation

One method that I, and athletes that I've coached, use is muscle tension and relaxation (MTR). Many people find it extremely difficult to relax, so much so that in their busy everyday lives, they can't even recognize when they are tense. MTR contrasts the extremes of tension and relaxing.

MTR exercise

1 Lie down on the floor in a comfortable position without crossing your arms or your legs (this may stop the blood flowing through the muscle groups properly).
2 Tense your muscles as tightly as you can and hold this contraction for seven seconds.
3 Release the tension.

Now it is very, very important that when you release the tension you do it **immediately** and **not** gradually. You will notice a complete difference in the way your muscles and body feel. This is because we have exaggerated both the tension and the relaxation. This is the starting point of the tension and relaxation exercise. Some people like to break down the MTR into a few muscle groups:

- face and neck
- arms and hands
- chest and shoulders
- stomach
- back
- backside
- upper and lower legs.

This is entirely up to you of course, and you should do whatever works best for you. It is worth repeating the MTR three times, with seven seconds of tension and then about 20–30 seconds total relaxation before repeating.

Control and separation

Another method of reducing anxiety and worry is to take control and plan as thoroughly as you possible can. It's important that you deal with things that can go wrong, both physically and mentally, in training. Play the 'What if...' game. What if I can't get my shoes on in transition? What if I can't get my shoe onto the pedal? What if I fall over on the corner? What if I'm boxed in coming into transition? What if I keep getting blocked as I'm trying to break away?

If you can't imagine what can go wrong – and practise dealing with such situations in training – then you won't develop strategies to deal with these occurrences. When something unfortunate happens, deal with it immediately and then move on. It is crucial that accidents are anticipated and you know what to do. Sometimes you might even think, 'Good, I'm glad this has happened because I know what to do and I can get it out of the way early in the race.' Anticipate that something will go wrong during the race and be prepared for it.

Turning negatives into positives

I used to coach a wonderful athlete, Sian Brice, who represented Great Britain in the 2000 Sydney Olympic Games. In that Olympic triathon in Sydney, Sian Brice was kicked in the face in the first 100 metres of the swim; her goggles were dislodged and filled with water, and she had enormous decisions to make. How she reacted was absolutely crucial. She reacted brilliantly and positively because she had practised things going wrong before in training, and had experienced negative things in previous races. In her first World Cup race some three years previously in Stockholm, she had also been kicked in the face and had lost her goggles completely – learning what to do then had made it an experience that, although not pleasant in Sydney, she was able to rationalize and deal with. Her mindset was, 'Well, it's happened, but I know what I have to do, I can put up with this discomfort for 20 minutes; this is the Olympics Games and far worse things can happen'.

Being mentally tough can sometimes mean that you're not a very nice person! This can mean that you come to dislike aspects of your character, which leads to a dilemma. The solution is to separate the person as a non-athlete and the athlete. When you are training or racing you have to think as an athlete; when you are away from triathlon you can separate yourself from this and from these attitudes.

Being mentally tough does not necessarily mean being in mental control. Anger, rage and frustration are strong indications of this. However having mental control will probably mean being mentally tough.

Self-confidence

There are a number of practical ways to learn to become mentally stronger, more confident and self-reliant. Many of these are simple:

- talking to an experienced coach or to teammates
- reading books and listening to tapes
- speaking with a sports psychologist
- teaching yourself and taking responsibility and personal control over situations.

Faking it

There is no doubt that entering and then racing your first triathlon can be a nerve-racking experience. Everyone around you seems to know everyone else, everyone seems happy. In particular, the successful athletes who are known to you always appear to have self-confidence. But things aren't always what they seem... of all those confident athletes, how many of them really do have it? Perhaps not nearly as many as it appears; many less confident athletes 'fake it'.

Impostor syndrome

Coming into a new activity, not always a sport, but often a new job where perhaps you feel that you are under-qualified, leads to a feeling of uncertainty, a feeling of not being quite up to the task, a feeling that somebody else should really be doing what you're doing. This is known as the **'impostor syndrome'**. It is a hidden form of low self-confidence where you feel that:

- your abilities are over-estimated by others (the 'I really don't deserve to be here' feeling)
- you will be 'found out'

- you are not as good an athlete as you seem
- you are where you are by false pretences.

157 mental attitude and confidence

09

The impostor syndrome explains many of the mental attributes that we've looked at in this chapter, feelings of:

- anxiety
- lack of self-confidence
- depression
- frustration
- and, importantly, not performing to the best of your abilities at (big) events.

Many athletes have these feelings, but are unable to rationalize (explain) them, and successful athletes also have these feelings. What we must do now is to find out the difference in how successful athletes deal with the impostor syndrome, and how they overcome these feelings. The difference is that with experience, they have learnt to edit out and ignore these negative messages. They may still feel like impostors, but they have created a strategy to overcome these feelings. Their trick is to carry on in spite of these feelings.

Top tip

Other athletes feel like this as well. There is *nothing* wrong with pretending to be more at ease in a situation than you really are. We know that increased self-confidence leads to better performance in both training and racing, and a lack of self-confidence is perhaps the single biggest reason for not going on to the 'next' level.

Mind games

There are many strategies – mind games if you like – that you can use to build self-confidence, overcome the impostor syndrome and negate the advantages of other athletes that you've built up in your mind.

Try these mind games:

- Remember that every single athlete on the starting line used to have their nappy changed by their mum and dad.
- Every single athlete on the starting line has had at least one pathetic performance.

- Every single athlete on the starting line has had one of 'those' races where everything has gone wrong.
- Ask yourself: 'What is the worst thing that can happen?'
- Say to yourself: 'Even if I drop out on the swim; crash on the bike; puncture on the bike; tie up completely and have to walk on the run, I will still survive, nothing will have changed in me as a person.'

Do not compare yourself with an athlete who looks great, looks fit and tanned, looks mean and lean, is wearing the latest clothing. If you make this comparison, what you are doing is comparing your **inside (feelings)** with their **outside (appearance)** and this is doomed to failure. This is being completely unfair to yourself. You are making the assumption that because someone *looks* good, they *are* good. What these athletes *are* good at, is promoting a *positive* image. **There is no reason why you should not do exactly the same.**

There is nothing worse than constantly making negative comparisons with the success of other athletes that you mix with. Your sporting circumstances are unique to you. Don't fix on one athlete in the group who always looks happier and has more competitive success than yourself. Remember that they will have their own problems and worries.

Think positive!

No more self-criticism, replace with PMA (positive mental attitude).

Do this every morning and evening:

- Imagine yourself as confident, successful, in control.
- Imagine training and racing how you would like to and because you want to.
- Imagine getting the success you deserve.
- Imagine dealing with difficult and challenging training and racing situations positively.

Just take two minutes at a time and see what happens.

Strategies to increase confidence and self-control

Use triggers

Associate self-confidence with a physical or mental or word 'trigger'. For example, these could be smiling, the word 'calm', any number of small, positive aspects that will make you feel good about yourself. When you have to deal with a challenging training/racing situation, increase your confidence by triggering the positive symbol or by saying the trigger word. This is just like physical training and conditioning, the more you do it, the better it will become.

Act 'as if'

Who's your hero? Who do you admire? How would they deal with this 'difficult' situation? Do what you think your hero would do, talk the way you think they would talk. Imagine that the athlete dealing with this difficult challenge is very assured (rather than you) and you will be far less scared of making mistakes. Behaving this way feeds on itself and you will become that self-assured athlete.

Physical appearance

Look good and you'll feel good. If you send yourself the message that you deserve the best, you deserve to look the best.

Top tips

When you feel good about yourself, reflect that inner pride and confidence to others by:

- ensuring you have good posture
- standing straight, walking tall
- keeping your shoulders back and down
- imagining one thread pulling your head upwards, another thread pulling your head forwards.

Don't worry about other athletes' approval

Many athletes use up a lot of energy worrying about what other people may think of them. Do what you think is best in training, don't worry that other athletes may be looking at your training and racing and criticizing. You can't make everyone happy... and why should you? Somebody will *always* think that you're doing it wrong. Just accept that's its okay for other athletes to criticize you, but that it doesn't matter a stuff to you.

Don't build things up in your own mind

If one small thing goes wrong, it isn't going to make a major difference to you. If one enormous thing goes wrong, that still doesn't mean the end of the world. Ask yourself, 'What's the worst thing that can happen?' You will work out that you can deal with it, whatever it is.

Learn from your mistakes and move on

Oops! Wrong! Guess what? You aren't perfect. You will make mistakes and do things wrong sometimes. Learn from the mistakes and move on. Be grateful for all the mistakes you might make; by doing things wrong, you will learn how to do them right next time. Some coaches say that FAIL stands for First Action In Learning.

Try your best – you can't do any more

Do every training session and every race to the best of your ability; even if it doesn't end up perfect, be proud that you tried. Be happy with what you did, rather than punish yourself for what you didn't do.

Top tips

When you are nervous try to improve your control by:

- slowing down your speech
- using a lower tone of voice
- making eye contact
- being aware of your breathing pattern – breathing deeply and slowly.

The outcome is that the message you send both to yourself and others is that **you are in control**.

However much hard work is put into physical training, without a strong mental attitude you will not achieve your potential. There are always things that go wrong, things to deal with that are not necessarily to do with training. There will be periods of little or no improvement during training, and this can be frustrating. A strong mental attitude will guide you through these 'down' times and help you to overcome any barriers that might hinder your performance on race day. The other 'non-training' element that can seriously affect your training and racing performance is your diet. Read on to find out more!

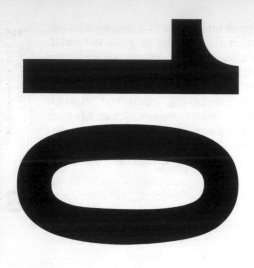

10

diet, nutrition and supplements

In this chapter you will learn:
- about getting energy from food
- the essentials of carbohydrate, fat and protein
- about fluid intake and dehydration
- about nutritional supplements.

Although having a good diet is no guarantee of success in triathlon, a poor diet may well be detrimental to performance in both training and racing. Your body is like a car, your mode of transport, and just as a car needs the correct fuel, so does your body. Good nutrition is fundamental to proper training and recovery. One of the nice things about exercising and training regularly is that it makes food more enjoyable! The additional exercise uses up more energy, which equals being able to eat more (you will need to eat more!) without gaining any extra weight.

If you don't eat properly then there is a chance that you will run out of energy during a training session or even in your first race, and that is something that you don't want to happen. You may even put yourself at risk of getting injured or falling prone to illness. Towards the end of this chapter there is a small section on supplements; it may well be that this doesn't interest nor seem applicable to you at the moment, however, it may well later on.

It is impossible to cover all aspects of diet and nutrition in one chapter, so if you are interested in reading more, check out the further reading section in Taking it further at the end of this book.

Energy and carbohydrate

The two factors in diet which will make training less enjoyable than it should be and will cause recovery to be slow are carbohydrate (glycogen) depletion and dehydration. During exercise the body takes its energy from carbohydrate (glycogen) stores in the muscles and liver. These energy stores are small, and will become gradually depleted during long, hard training sessions. This is likely to make you feel tired and lethargic, and will force you to slow down in training and racing. It is essential that the energy levels are maintained between training sessions by ensuring that the glycogen stores are filled. A diet with adequate carbohydrate is essential as the amount of glycogen you store is directly related to the amount of carbohydrate you consume.

> **How long can you go without refuelling?**
>
> We store enough carbohydrate in our liver and muscles to provide approximately 90 minutes worth of medium-intensity exercise. If you are resting or not working hard you will last longer without refuelling; if you have a really tough workout the fuel won't last as long. It can take up to 48 hours to fully refuel glycogen stores, so make sure you're not starting out half-empty by overtraining or not consuming enough carbohydrates.

However, this is not a green light to eat as much as you like. Any food that is not turned into energy will become fat, and is stored by the body and will cause weight gain. In triathlon and other long-endurance events, after about two hours of physical exertion you will be using much more fat than carbohydrate for fuel, but as fat does not completely break down without carbohydrate, you will need to take on more carbohydrate to top up your energy in the form of energy drinks.

Carbohydrate-rich foods

- rice
- pasta
- bread
- beans and pulses
- cereals
- potatoes and other vegetables
- fruit.

Fat

Fat is often seen as the 'bad' food. Wrong! There isn't any bad food, and it is wrong to try to completely exclude fat from your diet. A tremendous amount of energy is stored in fat, more than twice the amount found in carbohydrate or protein per gram. Fat also has other roles in the body: it insulates your body and cushions the vital organs such as the liver and kidneys; it is needed for the fat-soluble vitamins; and is involved in the formation of every cell membrane.

Foods containing fat

- butter and margarine
- oils
- sauces such as mayonnaise, salad cream and oil dressings
- meat and fish
- eggs (all the fat is in the yolk)
- full- and reduced-fat dairy foods (milk, yoghurt, cream)
- avocado, nuts and seeds.

Protein

Protein is used to build the cells in your body and to keep them healthy and functioning well; your muscles, bones, skin and hair need protein and it is essential to have some protein every day. Protein is not a preferred fuel source, but in times of need it can be converted into fuel to provide energy.

Protein-rich foods

- meat and fish
- eggs
- dairy foods (milk, yoghurt, cream)
- soya (tofu, soya milk and yoghurt)
- vegetable foods may also contain reasonable amounts of protein, particularly nuts, seeds, beans and pulses.

Appropriate eating

The triathlete should be aware of what is appropriate for training and exercising. Food high in carbohydrate (pasta, rice, potatoes, bread, cereals, vegetables and fruit) should make up a good proportion of your diet while foods with a high fat content (cakes and biscuits, fatty meat and food with a lot of cream or oil) should be kept at a low level.

A general rule of thumb is to make sure that your diet (or even each meal) is made up as follows:

- carbohydrate constitutes 50–60%
- protein 15–20%
- fat no more than 20%.

There is absolutely nothing wrong in having cream cakes, pizza and other 'bad' foods some of the time, the key is to eat them in moderation.

It is important to spread your meals throughout the day. Avoiding breakfast and then eating a big meal in the evening is not the way to go. Snacking or 'grazing' will keep carbohydrate levels up. Fresh fruit and vegetables are essential, the fibre content along with the minerals and vitamins necessary for healthy living make eating five portions each day a sensible habit.

Eating when training and racing

Individuals vary greatly in their tolerance to food eaten before exercise. Some athletes find it impossible to eat within three hours of training or competition while others can eat less than an hour before, although for the majority this is not to be advised. Eating during any triathlon from short sprint events up to and including Olympic distance events is not recommended. However, in any event lasting an hour or more you will need to take on water, and events lasting approximately two hours or more will require energy drinks to be consumed to top up carbohydrate levels. Individual tolerance also plays a part in what type of energy drinks can be taken on board during a race – remember to experiment in training rather than in races.

Any discomfort felt when taking in fluids can also be a symptom of dehydration, which makes it much harder for an athlete to absorb fluids and carbohydrate. Muscle glycogen is re-stocked more quickly if carbohydrate is taken in immediately after training and racing. If you find it difficult to eat, then you must at least drink instead. There are now many different brands of sports drinks which provide essential liquid and nutrition without the discomfort that some athletes find with food.

There are a number of self-checks that can be done to help with monitoring drinking and eating during and after training (see later in the chapter).

Water and dehydration

Water is essential to sustain life. It helps to transport nutrients and oxygen around your body and gets rid of waste matter through the kidneys. It lubricates your joints and your eyes, and is necessary for the chemical reactions in digesting your food. Water maintains blood pressure and aids our breathing.

Everybody needs between two and three litres of water every day, and athletes require more. In hot weather you sweat and lose water, and need even more water to ensure you don't become dehydrated. Try to get in the habit of carrying a water bottle everywhere you go so you can continually top up your water stores.

If you aren't going to the toilet at least every three hours, then you're probably not drinking enough. If you're not drinking sufficient water then it is possible that you will feel thirsty, tired and emotional, have headaches and tingling sensations in your hands. Feeling thirsty is not always a quick enough warning, so drink whether you're thirsty or not, as by the time you are thirsty, you may be dehydrated. Drink little and often, before, during and after exercise. Always start in a well-hydrated state.

Top tip

Dehydration will reduce your performance. If your body weight is just two per cent lower through dehydration (water loss), this can decrease your exercise performance by up to 20 per cent.

Dehydration danger signs

If you do succumb to dehydration without realizing it, there are a number of pointers which indicate it. You may feel tired and weak, your legs start to feel wobbly, you will have severe thirst and will be slowing down. These are frequently indicators of dehydration. If these symptoms do appear, you should take action immediately by stopping training and allowing your body to rest and recuperate.

Fluid loss and replenishment

A weight loss of one kilogram (just over two pounds) is very common during a training session and is equivalent to one litre of sweat (water) loss. You must drink to replenish this fluid loss. It is worthwhile checking your body weight occasionally before and after a training session and monitoring the difference. It is particularly important to check and be aware of this during swimming sessions. With your body immersed in water for an hour, there can be significant fluid loss without you realizing it. It is important to have a plastic water bottle by the side of the pool for every training session.

The urine test

You can tell if you are well hydrated through the colour of your urine. Your urine should be a very pale straw colour. If you are dehydrated, your urine will appear darker in colour and reduced in volume, and it may also smell quite strong. If your urine is anything other than a pale straw colour, you need to drink more fluids, ideally water.

Nutritional supplements

There are many products on the sports market that promise to give you a better, faster race. While you are relatively new to triathlon, be wary of the claims made for these products; if they did work as they say, then everybody would be taking them, which they are not.

Equally, there are a number of products that contain substances that are highly contentious, if not illegal – the so-called 'performance enhancing substances'. A rule of thumb that might well have some truth in it is: 'If it works, it's probably banned, if it's not banned, it probably doesn't work.' You may believe that this entire area does not affect you at the moment, however, the nature of our competitiveness means that athletes are always trying to set new personal best performances and it is easy to become susceptible to the claims made by performance enhancing aids. It is your responsibility to be aware of products and their contents; ignorance is no excuse.

Efficacy and ethics

Always ask the following questions when considering a nutritional supplement. Does it work? Who says so? Under what conditions has it been proven to work? Are the claims independent of the manufacturer or supplier? Has controlled, regulated testing been undertaken? Is its use in the sport legitimate? Some sports allow certain products while other sports do not – it is your responsibility to find out what is legal and allowed in your sport and in different events. There may also be an added complication that certain products may be legal to supply or sell, but illegal to take. Substances which are banned include Vitamex and Up your Gas.

Do they work or not?

Some well-known substances and supplements that have been proven not to have an ergogenic (performance enhancing) effect, despite claims being made as to their efficiency, include ginseng, bee pollen, gelatine, aspartate, ornithine and royal jelly. Some supplements that may possibly have an effect include the following:

- antioxidants
- arginine
- BCAA (branch chain amino acids)
- bicarbonate
- caffeine
- colostrums
- creatine
- glutamine
- Hydroxymethylbutyrate
- zinc.

Of course, you need to know the following about any substance before you decide to take it:

- What does it do in the body?
- Am I likely to be deficient in this nutrient/product? In other words, if I already have an optimum level of this from my diet, what would more do?
- How does it work?
- How much would I have to take, how often, and how long do the effects last?
- Are there any side effects or health risks?

Here is just a small amount of information on some of these sports performance aids.

Antioxidants

These include Vitamins A, C and E, carotenoids, flavenoids, polyphenols, glutathiane, lipoic acid, zinc and selenium. Antioxidants have many important roles in the body, including proper immune functioning and reduction of free radical damage caused by exercise. However, you are more likely to benefit from taking antioxidants if your diet is not providing an ample amount already. Make sure you fill up on brightly coloured fruits and vegetables, and include protein foods in the diet.

BCAA (Branch Chain Amino Acids) and glutamine

BCAA may be taken to reduce the likelihood of lean muscle being broken down for fuel, or to reduce feelings of fatigue, but the evidence is not convincing, and as long as you are eating sufficient protein you will have plenty of amino acids circulating in the bloodstream. Glutamine is an amino acid that has claims of enhanced performance attached to it. All amino acids are found in protein foods, so if you are consuming enough protein you will be taking in amino acids.

Bicarbonate

There is evidence that this works and there is fairly minimal discomfort. However, sadly for endurance athletes, improvement is noted over exercise and competition up to ten minutes only and is better suited for 800-metre, 1500-metre and 3000-metre running.

Caffeine

This well-known stimulant has often had ergogenic performance enhancing claims made in connection with it, and it is not tested out of competition. It is also a diuretic (something that prompts formation of urine and loss of water via the kidneys), though this can be overcome by ensuring water intake is ample. The diuretic effect (and the ergogenic effect) is likely to be reduced in regular coffee drinkers or in caffeine intake from tea, hot chocolate or cola drinks. There is evidence that caffeine does work in sprint and endurance events. Many athletes drink it one to three hours before exercise, but this is something you must try during training as we can all expect individual effects from any dietary source. Caffeine also affects perceived fatigue, so you will feel less tired.

Bovine colostrum

Colostrum is the first milk produced for newborn babies, and it is known to be extremely nutritious, also containing high levels of immunoglobulins for enhanced immune support (bovine means that it is from a cow). It is most likely to boost immune function for a short period, which may then stimulate the strength and speed that are claimed effects. However, there is also a theory that it may stimulate pre-cancerous cells.

Hydroxymethylbutyrate (HMB)

There is some evidence to suggest that this works, however, it can increase muscle mass by up to two kilograms in males, and up to one kilogram in females, which may well be detrimental to performance in endurance events.

So it seems that even when considering supplementation, it comes down to whether your normal daily diet is providing the nutrients you need to begin with.

Top tips

Each nutrient has many roles to play in the body, but where the triathlete is concerned, the most important factors are to ensure that you are:

- getting enough carbohydrate for energy
- staying well hydrated every day, during training and racing
- filling up depleted glycogen (carbohydrate) stores between training sessions
- eating balanced proportions of all food groups, including fibre, vitamins and minerals
- eating a healthy balanced diet containing lots of antioxidants
- eating sufficient protein to maintain good immune function and aid recovery: both essential for the serious athlete
- eating sufficient good fats in the diet (from nuts, seeds, oils, fish) which will provide additional energy and nutrients
- eating a little bit of what you fancy; this is fine considering the amount of training you are likely to be doing!

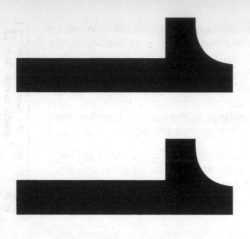

a six-month training schedule into your first race

In this chapter you will learn:
- how to plan your training programme
- how to progress gradually but effectively
- how to taper your training in the final week before the race.

All the advice, all the help and instructions will not mean anything unless you *do* something! It's translating those thoughts and good intentions into action that really count, that will make a difference to your life. Triathlon is a sport, but it is also very much a lifestyle that you choose. You choose to be active and fit, you choose to take part not in one sport but four: swimming, cycling, running and triathlon. It's a great choice to make, now *do* it!

This chapter provides the ultimate guide, the essential training programme that will lead you through six months of training, straight up to and into your first triathlon. Exciting, isn't it? Now it's time to really get started – arrange your first race for six months time perhaps?

If you need a reminder of any of the drills or exercises as you read through this chapter, just go back to the relevant chapters on swimming, cycling and running; everything that is set out here has been discussed earlier in the book.

Training schedule weeks 1–4

The cycle and run sessions are already slotted into the week, you just need to fit in the three weekly swim sessions underneath each table whenever you can. Don't worry too much about the order of doing each session through the week for this introductory period – you will be so busy trying to organize pool time and juggling the three disciplines that it will be very much a question of fitting the sessions in when time and facilities are available. The training programme and especially the days chosen, are just one option.

Swimming notes: For swimming particularly, don't start by emphasizing distance, just work on putting the time in. Swimming is a different skill, a different fitness, a different hurt! Again, the three essentials in swimming are technique, technique, and technique. Concentrate on easy, relaxed swimming and try to develop a 'feel' for the water. Look back at the swimming chapter for all the important points on technique, stroke and drills.

Cycling notes: For the cycling sessions, cadence (pedalling speed) is more important than brute force in the early stages, so try to work in a gear where you can pedal for at least 90+ revolutions per minute – it will pay dividends later. The majority of these sessions can be done at this stage on either the road, or on the turbo (wind trainer), or on an exercise bike in the gym.

Recovery times for all disciplines are shown in brackets for simplification.

Week 1

WEEK 1	MON	TUES	WED	THURS	FRI	SAT	SUN
CYCLE	30 mins steady		40 mins steady			50 mins steady	
RUN		20 mins steady		25 mins steady			40 mins steady

SWIM – Week 1
1 Swim 1 length (rest 10 seconds), repeat for 10 minutes or 400 metres. If okay, repeat for a further 5 minutes or 200 metres.
2 As above but count swim strokes for each length – if the number of strokes increase, it's a sign that technique is falling apart. If you are feeling strong, add another 5 minutes or 200 metres.
3 Time trial for 10 minutes and take total distance swam.

Week 2

WEEK 2	MON	TUES	WED	THURS	FRI	SAT	SUN
CYCLE	10 mins warm-up 5 × 1 min at 90% effort (1 min recovery in low gear) 10 mins warm-down		50 mins steady			75 mins steady	

WEEK 2 (Contd)	MON	TUES	WED	THURS	FRI	SAT	SUN
RUN		10 mins easy jog 10 × 30 secs at 80% effort (30 secs jog recovery) 10 mins jog warm-down		30 mins steady			45 mins steady

SWIM – Week 2

1 Similar to week 1 but swim 50 metres (10 seconds recovery after each 50 metres), repeat for 12 minutes or 600 metres. If OK, repeat for a further 8 minutes or 400 metres.

2 800-metre–1000 metre swim as 200-metre warm-up, then 4–6 repeats of 100 metres with 30 seconds recovery, 200-metre warm-down.

3 15 minute time trial and take total distance swam.

Week 3

WEEK 3	MON	TUES	WED	THURS	FRI	SAT	SUN
CYCLE	10 mins warm-up 5 × 2 mins at 90% effort (1 min recovery in low gear) 10 mins warm-down		60 mins steady			10 mins warm	

WEEK 3 (Contd)	MON	TUES	WED	THURS	FRI	SAT	SUN
RUN		10 mins easy jog 6 × 1 min at 80% effort (1 min jog) 10 mins jog warm-down		30 mins steady			50 mins steady

SWIM – Week 3

1 1000–1500-metre swim. This should be broken down into a 300-metre warm-up, then 5–10 repeats of 100 metres with 20–30 seconds recovery and 200-metre warm-down.

2 1500-metre swim consisting of 400-metre warm-up, then 3 × 100 metres with 30 seconds recovery (first 100-metre swim on full stroke, second 100-metre swim extending the stroke as long as possible, counting the strokes, and third swim as alternating 'ordinary' swimming and extending length of stroke. Repeat this 3–4 times. 100–400-metre warm-down.

3 20 minute time trial and take total distance swam.

Week 4

WEEK 4	MON	TUES	WED	THURS	FRI	SAT	SUN
CYCLE	5 mins warm-up 20 mins at 80% effort 5 mins warm-down		75 mins steady			90 mins steady	

WEEK 4 (Contd)	MON	TUES	WED	THURS	FRI	SAT	SUN
RUN		10 mins easy jog 5 × 90 secs @ 80% effort (1 min jog) 10 mins jog warm-down		30 mins steady			50 mins steady

SWIM – Week 4

1 Long swim for distance, no warm-up, just swim for 30 minutes and take total distance. This a mentally tough session the first time through.

2 Take one-quarter of the distance of the above session and attempt to swim the distance X times in less than 7 minutes each time. Take 2 minutes recovery between each.

3 Fartlek swim: 100 metres easy, 10 seconds recovery, 50 metres hard and repeat 8 times.

Training schedule weeks 5–8

Swimming notes: For all swimming sessions, however hard you're working, the number one priority is to maintain a good technique throughout. Count the number of strokes that you take for each length of the pool every length, every session. The first swim session of each week in this phase is a 'broken' 1500-metre swim to monitor your improvement.

Cycling notes: Remember to focus on cadence rather than big gears! More than 90 revolutions per minute is still the target. Also remember the majority of these sessions can still be done on either the road, or on the turbo (wind trainer), or on an exercise bike in the gym.

Week 5

WEEK 5	MON	TUES	WED	THURS	FRI	SAT	SUN
CYCLE	30 mins hard ride (time trial effort)		10 mins warm-up 5 × 90 secs out of saddle in hardest gear* (1 min) warm-down			90 mins steady ride	
RUN		20 mins hard run		10 mins easy jog 4 × 2 mins at 80% effort (1 min jog) 10 mins warm-down			50 mins

* You won't be able to hold 90 rpm cadence for this.

SWIM – Week 5

1 30 × 50 metres, 10 seconds rest after each 50 metes. Note the time.
2 As above but only 20 × 50 metres. Your aim is to take two strokes less for each 50 metres while maintaining the same times.
3 A 10-minute steady swim focus on technique, take 1 minute break and swim a further 10 minutes attempting to increase the distance covered.

Week 6

WEEK 6	MON	TUES	WED	THURS	FRI	SAT	SUN
CYCLE	60 mins steady ride		10 mins warm-up 10 × 1 min at 90% effort (1 min in low gear) 10 mins warm-down			75 mins steady ride	
RUN		5 mins easy jog 3 mins at 80% effort – keep speed up (1 min jog) 5 mins warm-down		10 mins easy jog 15 × 30 secs at 80% effort (30 secs jog) 10 mins warm-down			55 mins steady run

SWIM – Week 6

1 10 sets of 100 metres, 10–20 seconds rest, 50 metres, 10 seconds rest, and repeat 10 times to achieve 1500 metres. Note the time.
2 Power swim. After warm-up, swim 10 × 50 metres with 1 minute recovery between swims. Note the time. Warm-down.
3 Technique session. After warm-up swim 12 × 50 metres as follows:

Lengths 1, 4, 7, 9 – overemphasize body rotation, push side of hips towards bottom of pool

Lengths 2, 5, 8, 10 – overemphasize extending the stroke, as you change from pulling to pushing away, push hands away and keep in water as long as possible, think 'aim towards knees'

Lengths 3, 6, 9, 12 – high elbow, think of your hand and arm entering the water and then placing over a barrel under the water. No times taken.

Week 7

WEEK 7	MON	TUES	WED	THURS	FRI	SAT	SUN
CYCLE	35 mins hard ride		10 mins warm-up 3 × 1 min out of saddle in hardest gear* (1 min recovery) 2 mins out of saddle (1 min recovery) warm-down			90 mins steady ride	
RUN		10 mins easy jog 2 × 6 at 80% effort (2 mins jog) 10 mins warm-down		25 mins hard run			40 mins steady run

* You won't be able to hold 90 rpm cadence for this.

SWIM – Week 7

1 15 × 100 metres with 15 seconds break. Take times.
2 4 × 400 metres with 2 minutes recovery between. Try to hold the same 100-metre splits as on the broken 1500-metre swim.
3 Pure stroke swim. Swim 10 × 100 metres, no times taken; each rep concentrate on length of stroke, stroke count, body rotation, high elbow.

Week 8

WEEK 8	MON	TUES	WED	THURS	FRI	SAT	SUN
CYCLE	60 mins steady ride		5 mins warm-up 5 × 3 mins 90% effort (1 min) 5 mins warm-down			2 hour ride	
RUN				60 mins steady run			30 mins fartlek, at least 10 mins hard running

SWIM – Week 8

1 5 × 200 metres then 10–20 seconds rest, then 100 metres and 10 seconds rest. Repeat 5 times for 1500 metres. Note the time.
2 Power swim. After warm-up, swim 10 × 50 metres with 1 minute recovery between swims. Aim to equal times from previous power swim but to take two strokes less each 50 metres. Note the time. Warm-down.
3 Technique session. After warm-up swim 12 × 50 metres, swim lengths as follows:

1, 4, 7, 9 – overemphasizing correct hand and arm entry. Touch your thumb on outside of shoulder before entering water in a line between centre of forehead and shoulder body rotation, push side of hips towards bottom of pool

2, 5, 8, 10 – overemphasizing extending the stroke, as you enter the water keep pushing forwards further then you think you can before starting to pull back

3, 6, 9, 12 – high elbow, think of your hand and arm entering the water and then digging your fingers into a bucket of sand, securing a strong grip and pulling yourself forward. No times taken.

Training schedule weeks 9–12

Swimming notes: Remember that the priority for swimming is still to maintain a good technique throughout; stroke count, length of stroke, body rotation, high elbow. We continue with the first swim session of each week as a 'broken' 1500-metre swim, but the breaks are shorter. If a warm-up and warm-down is not specified, assume 400 metres of each. Use both for work on aspects of technique.

Cycling notes: Again, the focus is on cadence (unless we're working on hills or specifically big gearing); 100 rpm is the target for this month. Road, turbo, exercise bike, your choice.

Week 9

WEEK 9	MON	TUES	WED	THURS	FRI	SAT	SUN
CYCLE	90 mins– 2 hr steady ride		10 mins warm-up 4 × 1 min out of saddle (1 min recovery) warm-down			5 mins warm-up 25 mins hard ride (80%– 5%) 10 mins warm-down	
RUN		30 mins hard run		60 mins steady run			warm-up reducing recovery session

In the reducing recovery 200 metres session (or 30 second efforts), after each succeeding repetition take 15 seconds less rest; starting at 90 seconds and reducing through 75, 60, 45, 30, 15... If okay repeat, if still okay, repeat again. If still okay, you're not running hard enough! The rationale behind this session is that for triathlon, you're already tired when you start the run and this type of fatigue simulates that feeling, at least a little.

SWIM – Week 9

1 Swim, 50 metres, 100 metres, 150 metres, and 200 metres with 15 seconds break between each, and repeat the set 3 times for the 1500 metre total. Take time.
2 10 × 100 metres, alternating 95% effort on even numbers with a full emphasis on stroke technique on the even number repetitions, 15 seconds between repetitions.
3 12 minute steady swim focus on technique, take 1 minute break and swim a further 12 minutes attempting to increase the distance covered.

Week 10

WEEK 10	MON	TUES	WED	THURS	FRI	SAT	SUN
CYCLE	1 hr steady to hard ride		10 mins warm-up 12 × 1 min at 90% (1 min recovery) alternate big/small gears, 10 mins warm-down			90 mins –2 hr steady ride	
RUN		40 mins fartlek – at least 12 mins hard running		40 mins steady run			1 hr hills with jog-down recovery (10 mins easy jog)

SWIM – Week 10

1 5 × 300 metres, 15 seconds rest between for full 1500-metes. Note the time.

2 Power swim. After warm-up, swim 10 × 100 metres with 1 minute recovery between swims. Emphasis the second 50 metres of each swim and try to maintain stroke count when feeling tired. Note the time. Warm-down.

3 Technique session (similar to last month). After warm-up, swim 9 × 100 metres length as follows:

Lengths 1, 4, 7 – overemphasizing body rotation, push side of hips towards bottom of pool

2, 5, 8 – overemphasizing extending the stroke, as you change from pulling to pushing away, push hands away and keep in water as long as possible, think 'aim towards knees'

3, 6, 9 – high elbow, think of your hand and arm entering the water and then placing over a barrel under the water. No times taken.

Week 11

WEEK 11	MON	TUES	WED	THURS	FRI	SAT	SUN
CYCLE	first long time trial, 1 hr hard ride, note distance		90 mins– 2 hr steady ride			hill session*	
RUN				10 mins easy jog 3 × 5 mins at 80–5% (2 mins jog) 10 mins warm-down	30 mins steady run		60 mins steady run

* Hill session: 10 minutes warm-up, then 2 minutes out of the saddle, 1 minute spin recovery, 3 minutes out of saddle, 1 minute spin recovery, 4 minutes out of saddle, 1 minute spin recovery, 5 minutes out of saddle. Warm-down.

SWIM – Week 11
1 Swim 500 metre, 400 metre, 300 metre, 200 metre, 100 metre; 20 seconds break after each repetition for full 1500 metre distance. Note the times.
2 As last month, 4 × 400 metres with 2 minutes recovery between. Compare times to last month; there should be a significant improvement.
3 Pure stroke swim. Swim 12 × 100 metres (increase of two on last month), no times taken; each repetition concentrate on length of stroke, stroke count, body rotation, high elbow.

Week 12

WEEK 12	MON	TUES	WED	THURS	FRI	SAT	SUN
CYCLE			5 mins warm-up 6 × 3 mins at 90% (1 min recovery) 5 mins warm-down			2 hour ride including 1 hr hard ride in middle	
RUN				warm-up 20 × 30 secs hard (30 secs jog)			70 mins steady run

SWIM – Week 12

1 Swim 100 metres, 200 metres, 300 metres, 400 metres, 500 metres, 15 seconds rest for 1500 metres. Note the time.

2 Power swim (repeat session 5 from week 2). After warm-up, swim 10 × 100 metres with 1 minute recovery between swims. Emphasis on the second 50 metres of each swim and try to maintain stroke count – or even drop one stroke – when feeling tired. Note the time. Warm-down.

3 Technique session. After warm-up, swim 9 × 100 metres as follows:

Lengths 1, 4, 7 – overemphasizing correct hand and arm entry. Touch your thumb on outside of shoulder before entering water in a line between centre of forehead and shoulder body rotation, push side of hips towards bottom of pool

Lengths 2, 5, 8 – overemphasizing extending the stroke, as you enter the water keep pushing forwards further than you think you can before starting to pull back

Lengths 3, 6, 9 – high elbow, think of your hand and arm entering the water and then digging your fingers into a bucket of sand, securing a strong grip and pulling yourself forward. No times taken.

Training schedule weeks 13–16

Swimming notes: Think about technique; stroke count, length of stroke, body rotation, high elbow – use warm-up and warm-down for work on aspects of technique. The first swim session of each week is a 'broken' 1500-metre swim.

Cycling notes: Remember to aim (in general) for 100 rpm as cadence (unless we're working on hills or specifically big gearing); train on road, turbo or exercise bike.

Running notes: Now is the time to start introducing the skill and technique points (see Chapter 07) into each session. Maybe use the warm-up to focus on specific points, or incorporate the skills and drills into the entire session.

Week 13

WEEK 13	MON	TUES	WED	THURS	FRI	SAT	SUN
CYCLE	90 mins –2 hr steady ride		5 mins warm-up 30 mins hard ride 5 mins easy 30 mins hard ride aim for 80–5% 10 mins warm-down			10 mins warm-up 2, 3, 1, 3, 2, 3 mins out of saddle in hardest gear (1 min recovery between each) warm-down	

WEEK 13 (Contd)	MON	TUES	WED	THURS	FRI	SAT	SUN
RUN		35 mins hard run		60–70 mins steady run			Reducing recovery 200 metre run*

In the reducing recovery 200 metres session (or 30 second efforts), after each succeeding repetition take 15 seconds less rest; starting at 90 seconds and reducing through 75, 60, 45, 30, 15... If okay repeat, if still okay, repeat again. If still okay, you're not running hard enough!

SWIM – Week 13

1 Swim 750 metres, 500 metres, 250 metres with 15 seconds break between each for the 1500 metres total. Note the time.
2 200 metres fast followed by 100 metres emphasizing stroke technique. Repeat 5 times alternating 95% effort on 200 metres with a full emphasis on stroke technique on the 100-metre swims, 15 seconds between swims.
3 15 minute steady swim focus on technique, take 1 minute break and swim a further 15 minutes attempting to increase the distance covered.

Week 14

WEEK 14	MON	TUES	WED	THURS	FRI	SAT	SUN
CYCLE			10 mins warm-up 15 × 1 min at 90% (1 min		75 mins steady to hard ride	90 min–2 hr steady ride	

			recovery) alternate big/ small gears, 10 mins warm-down			
RUN		hills 60 secs+ up continue hard on flat 15 secs jog down recovery 10 mins warm-down	45 mins steady run			40 mins fartlek with 15 mins hard running, focus on speed

SWIM – Week 14

1 3 × 500 metres, 15 seconds rest between for full 1500 metres. Note the time.

2 Power swim. After warm-up, swim 3 × 4 × 100 metres with 30 seconds recovery between swims, 1 minute after each set of four. Emphasis the second 50 metres of each swim and try to maintain stroke count when feeling tired. Note the time. Warm-down.

3 Technique session again! After warm-up swim 12 × 100 metres as follows: Lengths 1, 4, 7, 10 – overemphasizing body rotation, push side of hips towards bottom of pool

Lengths 2, 5, 8, 11 – overemphasizing extending the stroke, as you change from pulling to pushing away, push hands away and keep in water as long as possible, think 'aim towards knees'

Lengths 3, 6, 9, 12 – high elbow, think of your hand and arm entering the water and then placing over a barrel under the water. No times taken.

Week 15

WEEK 15	MON	TUES	WED	THURS	FRI	SAT	SUN
CYCLE			Repeat long time trial ride (1 hr), note distance – aim is 5% more than last month		90 mins–2 hr steady ride	hill session as below*	
RUN	35 mins hard run			60–70 mins steady run			10 mins easy jog 4–5 mins at 80–5% 10 mins warm-down

* Hill session: 10 minutes warm-up, then 2, 4, 1, 3, 2, 4 minutes out of saddle with 1-minute spin recovery only. Take 3 minutes after the fourth effort (3 minute effort). Warm-down.

SWIM – Week 15

1 Swim 2 × 750 metres, 30 seconds break for full 1500 metre distance. Note the times.
2 100 metres at 95%, 10 seconds recovery only then 400 metres at 80% effort working on technique. Take 2 minutes rest and repeat twice more. This session is designed to simulate the discomfort you'll feel when going out hard in an open water swim.
3 Stroke swim. Swim 15 × 100 metres (increase of three on last month), no times taken; each rep concentrate on length of stroke – work now on the final push-away at end of stroke, stroke count, body rotation, high elbow.

Week 16

WEEK 16	MON	TUES	WED	THURS	FRI	SAT	SUN
CYCLE			5 mins warm-up 5 × 4 mins at 90% (1 min recovery) 5 mins warm-down			2 hour ride including 1 hr hard ride in middle	
RUN				warm-up 20 × 35 secs hard* (25 secs jog)			75 mins steady run

* For recovery make sure that you don't tail right off. This could be the session where you use each 35 second effort to concentrate on one particular aspect of your running.

SWIM – Week 16

1 Swim 1000 metres, 20 seconds recovery then 500 metres for 1 500 metres. Note the time.
2 Power swim. After warm-up, swim 12 × 100 metres with 45 seconds recovery between swims (take extra minute rest after 6 swims if absolutely necessary). Emphasis the second 50 metres of each swim and try to maintain stroke count – or even drop one stroke – when feeling tired. Note the time. Warm-down.
3 Technique session. After warm-up swim 12 × 100 metres as follows:

Lengths 1, 4, 7, 10 – overemphasizing correct hand and arm entry. Touch your thumb on outside of shoulder before entering water in a line between centre of forehead and shoulder body rotation, push side of hips towards bottom of pool

Lengths 2, 5, 8, 11 – overemphasizing extending the stroke, as you enter the water keep pushing forwards further than you think you can before starting to pull back

Lengths 3, 6, 9, 12 – high elbow, think of your hand and arm entering the water and then digging your fingers into a bucket of sand, securing a strong grip and pulling yourself forward. No times taken.

Training schedule weeks 17–20

You're not too far away now from that first race, but do remember to still focus upon your swimming technique:

- stroke count
- length of stroke
- body rotation
- high elbow.

Also, after examining running technique last month, remember that running is a skill, and time used to perfect technique won't be wasted.

Two new things to look at this month:

1 Open water swimming. Do not swim alone!
2 Back-to-back training – Note training different disciplines on the same day... easy does it to start with!

Cycling notes: Remember to aim for 100 rpm as cadence.

Week 17

WEEK 17	MON	TUES	WED	THURS	FRI	SAT	SUN
CYCLE	50 mins ride		5 mins warm-up 20 mins hard ride 5 mins easy 15 mins hard ride 5 mins easy 10 mins hard ride warm-down		90 mins–2 hr steady ride	10 mins warm-up 5 × 3 mins out of saddle, hardest gear (1 min recovery) warm-down	
RUN	30 mins run			reducing recovery 200 metre run*			60–70 mins steady run

* Repeat last month's session after warming up. Reducing recovery 200 metres session (or 30 second efforts): after each succeeding repetition take 15 seconds less rest; starting at 90 seconds and reducing through 75, 60, 45, 30, 15... If okay repeat, if still okay, repeat again. If still okay, you're not running hard enough! The rationale behind this session is that for triathlon, you're already tired when you start the run and this type of fatigue simulates that feeling, at least a little.

SWIM – Week 17

1 Swim 500 metres, then 1000 metres with 15 seconds break between each for the 1500 metres total. Note swim times.
2 6 × 200 metres as first 100 metres emphasizing stroke technique, straight into 100 metres fast with 60 seconds between swims.

3 Open water swim. Wear your wetsuit. Very easy introduction, try to stay in the water for 15 minutes, don't go too far away from the shore line, you must swim or be accompanied by/with someone (ideally have a friend accompanying you in a boat).

Week 18

WEEK 18	MON	TUES	WED	THURS	FRI	SAT	SUN
CYCLE			10 mins warm-up 10 × 2 mins 90% (1 min recovery) low gear) alternate big/small gears 10 mins warm-down		90 mins – 2 hr steady ride		60 mins steady ride
RUN	hills 5 × 60 secs + up, continue hard on flat 15 secs jog down recovery 10 mins warm-down			45 mins steady run			30 mins fartlek, first 3 mins focus on speed and cadence

SWIM – Week 18

1 Swim the full 1500 metres. Note the swim time.
2 Swim 4 × 400 metres hard, 2 minutes recovery between efforts.
3 Technique session. After warm-up, swim 12 × 100 metres alternating one very hard swim with one swim focusing on what you think is your *worst* point of technique. Then try to incorporate the corrections into the hard swims. 1 minute recovery between efforts. No times taken.

Week 19

WEEK 19	MON	TUES	WED	THURS	FRI	SAT	SUN
CYCLE			repeat long time trial ride (1 hr), note distance, aim is 5% more than last month		sprint session		2 × 30 mins ride as brick session with run
RUN	1 hr steady run			10 mins easy jog 4 × 6 mins 80–5% (90 secs jog) 10 mins jog warm-down			2 × 20 mins run as brick session with bike

SWIM – Week 19

1 Swim 15 × 100 metres, with 10 seconds between efforts and 30 seconds after each set of five efforts. Note swim times.

2 As last month; 100 metres at 95%, 10 seconds recovery only then 400 metres at 80% effort working on technique. Take 2 minutes rest and repeat twice more. This session is designed to simulate the discomfort you'll feel when going out hard in an open water swim.

3 Stroke swim (similar to last month). Swim 15 × 100 metres, first 3 swims as 95% effort, then 9 swims focusing on stroke (again!), and final 3 swims as 100% effort. Recover for 60 seconds between hard swims, 20 seconds between stroke swims.

Week 20

WEEK 20	MON	TUES	WED	THURS	FRI	SAT	SUN
CYCLE		5 mins warm-up 5 × 5 mins at 90% (1 min recovery) 5 mins warm-down				Use turbo, 4 × 8 mins steady ride as brick session with run rest 3 mins between each set	
RUN			warm-up 20 × 40 secs hard (20 secs jog)*	60 mins steady run		4 × 4 mins hard run as brick session with bike	

* This could be the session where you use each 35 second effort to concentrate on one particular aspect of your running.

SWIM – Week 20

1 Swim 5 × 300 metres, recovery as 45 seconds after first swim, then 30 seconds, 20 seconds and finally 10 seconds after fourth swim.
2 Open water swim. Swim non-stop for 10 minutes (parallel to the shore), rest 1 minute treading water then swim back faster. Use this swim to practise sighting to make sure that you swim in a straight line. At the end of swim, simulate transition by getting out of your wetsuit as quickly as possible.
3 Speed session. 3 × 4 × 100 metres, 1 minute recovery between each 100 metres; 3 minutes recovery after each set of four. Aim for 95% effort and try to maintain pace throughout.

Training schedule weeks 21–23

Just four weeks to go now! It's easy to panic and think of all the sessions that you didn't manage to do... why not instead think of all those that you did do? Remember to keep working on technique (particularly in swimming), and not to let your form suffer when you get tired.

So far, for all these training sessions, we have set out the three sessions for each discipline each week but left it to your decision as to when to do the training sessions if you couldn't stick to the suggested days. For the first two weeks of this final section (and the start of week 23), we have continued that process; however, if we're going to be serious about getting the best possible performance for the target race, then we need to taper, to prepare the best possible way that we can. Therefore, the last few days are structured – with sessions to do on each day – quite specifically. Try to follow these... if you can't, then work out what is best for you so that you can get to the race rested and prepared.

Mental preparation

• Think about the race through the final 7–10 days.
• Think about how hard you've worked for it.

197
a six-month training
schedule into your first race
11

- Think about all the things you've given up so that you were able to train for this.
- Think about how good you'll feel when you've finished.
- Think how you'll reward yourself when you've finished.
- Think about all those people who said you couldn't do it... it's partly because of them that you can!

Week 21

WEEK 21	MON	TUES	WED	THURS	FRI	SAT	SUN
CYCLE		5 mins warm-up 1 hr hard ride 5 mins warm-down		10 mins warm-up 4 × 6 just faster than race pace (1 min recovery) warm-down		Use turbo or exercise bike 4 × 5 km ride (12 mins) as brick session with run rest 2 mins between each set	
RUN			warm-up 20 × 30 secs fast strike (30 secs jog) 5 mins warm-down	75 mins steady run		4 × 1 km run as brick session with bike Warning tough session!	

SWIM – Week 21

1 Swim straight 1500 metres. Note the swim time.
2 1 × 400 metres, 2 × 200 metres, 4 × 100 metres still emphasizing stroke technique, one minute between efforts.
3 Open water swim. Wear your wetsuit again and stay in the water for 25 minutes non-stop swimming. Don't forget the safety aspects.

Week 22

WEEK 22	MON	TUES	WED	THURS	FRI	SAT	SUN
CYCLE		10 mins warm-up 15 × 1 mins at 90% (1 min recovery) 10 mins warm-down		90 mins –2 hrs steady ride		Use turbo or exercise bike 4 × 5 km ride at race pace as brick session with run rest 3 mins between each set	
RUN			hills, 6 × 60 secs + up, continue hard on flat 30 secs jog down recovery 10 mins warm-down	hard pace 30 mins run		4 × 1 km run as brick session with bike, try to run each km faster than the previous one	

SWIM – Week 22

1 750-metre swim, 1 minute recovery and then a further 750 metres, aiming to swim faster than the first 750 metres.

2 5 × 200 metre hard, 30 seconds only between efforts.

3 Technique session. Repeat of last month. After warm-up, swim 12 × 100 metres alternating one very hard swim with one swim focusing on what you think is your *worst* point of technique. Then try to incorporate the corrections into the hard swims. Take 1 minute recovery between efforts. No times taken.

Week 23

WEEK 23	MON	TUES	WED	THURS	FRI	SAT	SUN
CYCLE		40 mins time trial ride		3 × 8 mins on turbo or road faster than race pace (2 mins recovery)		4 × 4 mins cycling faster & harder than previous 8 min efforts rest 2 mins between each set	
RUN	60 mins steady run		10 mins jog 2 × 1.5 miles at 90% effort (2 mins jog recovery) 10 mins warm-down		8 × 1 min hard run (1 min jog recovery)	1 hour steady run	

SWIM – Week 23

1 Swim 1 × 500 metres, 5 × 100 metres, 10 × 50 metres with 3 minutes after the 500 metres and the 100 metres and 1 minute between the 50-metre swims. Focus on good quality swims and note your swim times.

2 Open water swim: 5 minutes easy warm-up then alternate 12 very hard fast strokes with 12 very easy long strokes; go through 10 times each. Then, 3 minutes easy swim then alternate 12 fast strokes breath-holding with 12 strokes easy, breathing every 2 strokes, go through 10 times each. 3 minutes easy warm-down.

3 300 metres, 200 metres, 100 metres and then repeat. Take 30 seconds only after the 300 metres and 200 metres and try to increase speed. Take 3 minutes after the first set. Maintain a good stroke and technique.

Now we are into the final week of our race preparation, we introduce another technique into our training schedule – tapering.

Tapering

Tapering is a specific method of training technique immediately prior to an important race. Essentially, it is a reduction in training, but it is how that training is reduced that is crucial to your race. It is the final phase of training and involves a reduction in training load by changing one or more of the following:

- time
- intensity
- frequency
- duration.

A good taper is aimed at stopping and reversing the fatigue that occurs during heavy training. Good tapering will also ensure that you do not lose any fitness going into the race.

A successful taper will improve physiological and psychological preparation, but requires very careful planning in order for it to be efficient. When you are working hard in the various phases of training, your body is continually stressed and in a constant state of tiredness and fatigue. As you become fitter, extra training sessions are added to the workload and even more stress is applied to your body, until it becomes accustomed to the new training load. Taking time away from training gives you and your body time to recover from all the hard work and be ready to face the next increase in the amount and intensity of training. This is the basis of tapering – rest allows recovery. However, the exact nature of the taper will be a great factor on the level of performance.

Do I need to taper?

It is important to state that not everybody responds well to tapering; not everybody needs to taper equally, and not everybody needs to taper in the same way and with the same methods. If you do not train very hard, then you probably do not need to taper at all – your body is already rested! However, starting triathlon training from nothing means that your body will, at least in the early stages, be extremely tired. As you become fitter and train more, how you and your body adapt to each increase in training load will decide whether you will need a short or long taper, or even if you need to change your training at all going into a race. Some lucky people seem to have the inborn genetic ability to be always able to recover quickly and fully from every training session.

The period of time needed to taper will vary depending on you as an individual; your height, size and weight, age and experience will all have a bearing on your taper. Too long a taper period will cause you to lose fitness as the training workload is decreased over too long a period of time, while too short a taper will not allow you sufficient time for full physiological and psychological recovery. As with all aspects of training, ideally tapering before a race should be a tried and tested method.

Types of tapering

There are many different types of taper of which three seem to be the most popular:

- Rest Only Taper (ROT)
- Low Intensity Taper (LIT)
- High Intensity Taper (HIT).

With the **rest only taper (ROT)**, the athlete merely stops all training some time before the race and rests. The period can be as little as two days or as much as two weeks.

With the **low intensity taper (LIT)**, all quality and high intensity training is stopped and training consists of easy swimming, cycling and running.

With the **high intensity taper (HIT)**, the athlete maintains or even increases the intensity but, importantly, reduces the actual time spent training.

Top tip

Athletes of all standards (including newcomers to triathlon) have performed well and badly with all these methods, however, most research and indicators show that the HIT is the most successful while the LIT makes little or no difference to a race performance and ROT will actually reduce race performance.

Successful tapers are generally high intensity, and so duration and/or frequency of training sessions must be lower if the overload workload is to be reduced. This is essential for sufficient rest and recovery between sessions and during sessions. The effective HIT must also be progressive within itself; the amount of time spent training is reduced each day and the intensity increases at the same time.

Physiological changes to your body during the tapering period

The physiological changes that take place in a high intensity taper will have the following effects:

- an increase in maximum oxygen uptake
- an increase in diameter and cross-sectional area of muscle fibres
- an increase in muscle glycogen (carbohydrate energy) storage
- an increase in strength and power.

The sum of these changes is that you will be rested and ready to race to the best of your ability, and, very importantly, you will enjoy the experience!

These physiological changes in your body along with psychological changes (see Chapter 09) will normally give improvements in racing performance. However, it is important to remember that there are great differences in adaptation and improvements between individuals. As a new triathlete, it is essential that you listen to your body and that you are prepared to make changes in your tapering if one method hasn't led to the expected and required results. Do remember, however, that as you become more experienced, there is little point in tapering for every event and race. If you do try this, you will lose too much training time and lose fitness as the season progresses. Again, do remember that the reaction of your body to any tapering programme will be specific to you as an individual.

So, let's take a look at that final week training schedule.

Week 24 – final training programme with tapering

Week 24 – Final taper week

WEEK 20	6 DAYS OUT	5 DAYS OUT	4 DAYS OUT	3 DAYS OUT	2 DAYS OUT	1 DAYS OUT	RACE DAY
SWIM		swim session (first session of week 4)			swim session (second session of week 4)	easy swim 10–15 min	have the best possible race, you deserve it!
CYCLE	10 × 1 hard (1 min recovery)		cycle 1 hour		cycle 30 mins with 6–8 faster sections for 30 secs recovery as required		

205
a six-month training
schedule into your first race **11**

Top tips

If you are planning a high intensity taper, consider the following points:

- Know what has and hasn't worked previously.
- Maintain or increase training intensity to greater than or equal to competition intensity.
- Reduce training volume by between one-third and half as the taper period starts, and between a further half and one-third as the taper period ends going into the race.
- Keep training frequency at least at three-quarters of normal amount but reduce time in each training session.
- Find out how many days taper your body requires (a lot of research indicates ten days before the event).
- Increase the recovery time between sets and repetitions.
- Find out what works for you as an individual.
- After the race, assess what worked well and what worked badly and use for future tapers.

As you become more involved in triathlon, tapering can be difficult psychologically, as you have become accustomed to training hard and for long periods of time. Some people find that they are reluctant to rest at all, as they feel that they will lose fitness almost instantly. This fear may not be well founded but even so, it can still be significant for the individual. If you find that this applies to you, then it may help to consider a longer warm-up and warm-down. This will allay the fear of losing volume as the overall distance stays steady by adding more to the warm-up and warm-down. A longer warm-up and warm-down will also reduce injury risk, which is important when the training session itself is of a higher intensity.

Other considerations in the week before the race

Sleeping

You are likely to have more energy and be less tired during your tapering week, so sleeping may become difficult, especially as race day comes closer. Don't worry about this; just try to rest as much as possible. If sleeplessness persists over a long period of time there are a variety of relaxation strategies that can be learnt (see Chapter 09).

Eating and drinking

You will have more time on your hands and may be tempted to eat more or continually sip at tea, coffee or sports drinks. Don't! The right nutrition becomes even more important as your event becomes imminent. You might find that you don't need to eat quite so much as your training tapers, but this is a good time to replenish carbohydrate stores and make sure that you have enough energy stored for your race.

Mental preparation

Focus on your race. Mentally go through every aspect of what may happen. Think about the transitions. Be prepared for every eventuality, and if and when it does occur, give yourself a pat on the back for not letting it be a surprise.

So, race day is finally here. Don't let all those months of hard training go to waste because you fail to think about the practical aspects of the triathlon event. Now relax, and start to make your lists of what you need and what you need to do on race day... it's all in the final chapter.

12

preparation for race day

In this chapter you will learn:
- how to prepare for race day
- what to do on race day
- about immediate pre-race preparation.

For some people, triathlon training is all about keeping fit, and these people might ask why do you need to race? The short answer is – you don't! However, having something to train for, a goal to achieve, is one of the most important things to keep you going. Without a goal, all that training can sometimes seem to be pointless. Racing fulfils that objective.

New athletes get nervous, and none more so than new triathletes. Triathlon can still seem to be a daunting challenge with all the variables it has, all the transitions and changes. If you are one of those people who get very nervous, one way of dealing with nerves is to focus on the time after the race, rather than the race itself. What will you tell your friends? How will they react to you being a triathlete? How good will you feel about yourself when you've completed a triathlon? These things are important, and can be a big factor in ensuring that not only do you race, but that you race well.

Your first triathlon is something special; it's something that sets you apart from 99 per cent of the population. It is your chance to show how hard you've worked and what you've already achieved. Taking part and finishing your first triathlon is one of those things that you will remember all your life. And there are so many things that we can do in the final few days, and on race day itself, that will help you to have your best possible race.

Things to consider

Before we look at all the positive things we can do to race well, let's take a look at things that can go wrong and how best to avoid them.

Many triathletes continue to train too hard going into a race – you can avoid this by tapering your training. However, there are other things to consider as well:

- suffering from nerves (see Chapter 09 on how to get a positive mental attitude!)
- incorrect food
- lack of sleep
- travelling too close to the race
- not knowing the course properly
- not knowing your actual starting time
- inappropriate, lost or forgotten kit and equipment.

The preparation for your first race really started the day you began training for triathlon; the final preparation begins a week before. For your race, you want to feel as good as you possibly can; fit, relaxed and confident.

Top tip

Make a timetable or timeline checklist and go through it step by step in the lead-up to your event. Following a timetable gives a sense of order to preparations and takes away a lot of nervousness.

Timeline checklist

The weekend prior to the race

- Do an early check on your bike and your race kit.
- Check brakes, steering, tyre pressure and tyres for cuts and small bits of glass.
- If the race is a long distance away, make sure that you have booked accommodation – telephone just to check that they have your reservation.
- Check the race destination with a map and ensure that you know the directions and the likely time it will take to get there.
- Make sure you know how you are getting there!

The day before race day

- Plan what you will eat for breakfast and all other pre-race meals the next day, and check that you have all these things in the cupboard! Race day is not the time to run out of porridge if that is your training and racing staple!
- Ensure that you have all the necessary clothes and equipment packed.

Top tip

Don't forget your essentials for race day. For immediately before the race, make sure that you have warm clothing, a water bottle to keep hydrated, an energy snack in case you have been too nervous to eat breakfast properly, and your race details.

Things you need for the race itself

Swimming

- wetsuit (if open water)
- swimming costume
- goggles
- swim hat (even if you expect the race organizers to supply one)
- towel (if you plan to use one quickly or stand on it)

Cycling and running

- racing bike
- crash hat
- top to wear for cycle and run disciplines (same one or two different ones)
- cycle shorts and running shorts (are you going to wear these or stay in a swimming costume?)
- cycle shoes and running shoes (with velcro, lacelocks or elastic laces)
- safety pins to pin your number on
- puncture repair kit
- cycle pump
- water bottles (one to go on your bike and one for transition)
- plastic bags for wet clothing
- Vaseline and talcum powder (for shoes and wetsuit)

After the race

- tracksuit or warm clothes
- something to eat and drink
- maybe some money to buy food, drink or browse the stands often at races.

The afternoon and evening before the race

Check out the race information pack and go to the pre-race briefing (these are sometimes immediately prior to the race on shorter sprint triathlons). Be sure to check what time your race start is. Remember, there may be as many as 20 different start times if it is a large event, and you alone will be responsible for getting to the start on time. If you do have any questions don't be afraid to ask them, but do check that they're not already answered in the race pack; athletes hate hearing questions asked when a little bit of reading would have already answered them.

Top tip

Be sure that you know the routes for all three disciplines by reading the race pack information and looking at the maps. If you have a chance and you get to the race venue early enough, it's worth driving around the cycle course; you may be able to drive around the run course as well if it's accessible. It is worth asking if there are any unusual aspects of the course. Essentially, ensure that you know whether the bike course is open (normal traffic will be operating) or closed to traffic during the race.

Try to take it easy in the afternoon and evening before the race – you'll feel nervous, but tell yourself that it's good nerves. Have a meal but try not to have anything too heavy on the stomach. If you can, stay with your normal food as much as possible. There's no point in changing to a bowl of pasta the night before the race just because other people have advised it; stay with the food you know – any radical adjustment will not do any good and may even be detrimental. If you have to travel and stay overnight, be sure you can get something acceptable to eat. If in any doubt, take your own food.

Getting a good night's sleep may be unlikely whether you're at home or in a hotel, but do try to rest. Relax, watch television or listen to music. Many triathletes think that it's not the sleep the night before the event, but rather two nights before that is important. You'll probably be at home two nights before, so a good sleep should be easier.

Make sure your water bottles are filled up. Put one in your bike bottle cage and the other one or two in your rucksack for carrying and transition. Put race numbers on your bike (find out where this should be fixed), and on your race top (or have the number on elastic if acceptable. It's important that you don't cut or change the numbers in any way.

Race morning

Most races in Britain have early morning starts so a lie-in is highly unlikely. It really isn't worth working out just how long you dare to stay in bed – you'll probably be awake before the alarm goes anyway. Give yourself enough time to wake up properly and get to the race in adequate time. If you have to drive and park at the race venue, make sure you know where the race parking is and if there are any restrictions.

Breakfast on race day

Eat breakfast. Even if you're nervous, you must have something – if you struggle to eat anything, try a banana and fruit smoothie. This can provide you with valuable carbohydrates. Your breakfast choice should depend upon the start time and length of the race. Follow these golden rules:

1 Eat something familiar that you know won't upset your stomach.

2 Drink, drink and drink again. Water is best but contrary to popular opinion, one cup of tea or coffee will not do you any harm.

3 Eat slow-release carbohydrates if you have a few hours before race time (porridge, beans on wholemeal toast), and faster-release carbohydrates (fruit smoothie, juice, breakfast cereals, white bread toasted) if you have less time before you start.

You will need to be number marked. This is for identification in case of accidents or if there are any disqualifications. Usually your leg and perhaps your arm will be marked. Don't leave this too late as you will get nervous if you're still lining up when your race start time is being called. Bike and helmet checks may also be carried out while you are registering or when checking your bike into the transition area.

Even with perfect pre-race preparation, things have a habit of taking longer than you anticipate so give yourself more time than you think you'll need. It's worth making out a timed list for your first race and trying to stick to it.

Don't forget the toilets! Race venue toilets have a habit of being particularly busy before an event; there are a lot of nervous athletes around. It can be useful to take spare toilet paper with you as this has a habit of running out! Know where the toilets are located and also find out if there are any alternative toilets nearby.

If you wear glasses...

If you wear prescription glasses, the race organizer may arrange for you to put them on a table on poolside, or will allow a race official to pass them to you as you exit the swim. If possible, put a small sticker with your race number on the side of your glasses. Straps can also be purchased which will hold your glasses firmly in place while cycling and running.

Setting up your kit in the transition area

Take as much time as you need to set up your own spot in transition. Stand there and mentally visualize exactly what you will do and what routine you will follow. There won't be much space, but that will be the same for everybody.

- Rack your bike where your race number is and check the tyre pressure one last time.
- The gears on your bike should be set low enough so that you can pedal easily at the beginning of the cycle discipline as soon as you are out of transition.
- Don't forget to leave a water bottle on your bike.
- Now set out your clothing and shoes.
- Finally, walk through the routes you will take in the transition areas, checking the entrance and exit for the swim, cycle and run.

Warming up before the race

Do you need to warm up? Most runners, swimmers and cyclists do warm up. Triathlon is a little different: if you warm up for the cycle and run, you still have to do the swim first. If you do decide to warm up for the cycle and the run, try this:

- do an easy 10–15 minute easy spinning ride
- incorporate two sprints of 30 seconds each
- then do a short jog, again with two short sprints of 30 seconds each
- if you're used to stretching before you swim, cycle or run, then you should do your stretches once you are warm.

To stretch or not to stretch?

We haven't discussed stretching before in this book. There are many different views on the value of stretching both before and after training and racing. Many experienced athletes have a standard procedure for stretching; equally, many experienced athletes prefer not to stretch at all. Stay with what you're accustomed to and if you do want to stretch, you must decide if you want to do this at race site or before you get there.

When you've finished your warm-up, go back to transition and re-check all your kit and equipment. Keep sipping from your water bottle to ensure that you've had enough water.

Now for your swim warm-up. Usually race organizers require you to warm up behind the start. Just stretch out into a long comfortable stroke, get used to the cold (if outdoors) and feel the water getting into your wetsuit and warming up your body. Again, a few short accelerations will ensure that the opening speed of the start isn't a surprise. Check your goggles for fit, make sure they don't leak or fog up.

Be at the water's edge/start line in plenty of time. Triathlons normally start in age-group waves, so check your wave start and look for swim hats the same colour as yours to ensure you're in the correct wave start. Stretch your shoulders and upper body, and roll your neck to reduce any tension. Decide where you're going to position yourself and stick with that decision; if you're a weak swimmer it's better to be at the side or at the end to minimize panic; if you're a strong swimmer then go to the middle of the front row.

Mental preparation

Before the race

Are you the type of person who needs to be around all the action? Or, do you like calmness and quiet before a race? It's your choice and you must choose what is appropriate for you, not what everyone else appears to be doing. Again, focus on what you will do. In your mind, go through the start, the swim, first transition, the bike, second transition, the run, the finish.

Also think about how much training you've done, and think of all the things that you've given up so you've been able to train for this event.

Make yourself mentally strong and positive about the race. First, try to relax (squeezing the shoulders and fists as tightly as you can and then instantly relaxing can help), then imagine yourself doing well in the actual race. Tell yourself... 'I'm really looking forward to this', 'I have prepared extremely well and I'll be able to cope with the weather and course conditions', 'I will finish this race', 'I will race my own race and not let anyone or anything distract me'.

After the race

Enjoy the feeling! You're a triathlete! Nothing can take that away from you.

In your euphoria don't forget to drink some water immediately and eat something to replenish your energy stores, within 20 minutes if possible. Put on warm, dry clothing and walk or jog easily for a few minutes. If you can bear to stretch, do that as well, it will pay dividends the following day.

Having done this you can think back on what you've done and what you had to do in preparation for it. Revel in your achievement.

And now... enter your next race!

taking it further

Books

Trew, S. 1990, *A Long Day's Dying,* Peterborough; Crowood Press

Trew, S. 2001, *Triathlon: A Training Manual,* Peterborough; Crowood Press

Trew, S. 1998, *Triathlon: The Skills of the Game,* Peterborough; Crowood Press

Trew, S. 2001, *A Moment of Suffering,* Essex, Wednesday Press

Bean, A. 1993, *The Complete Guide to Sports Nutrition,* London: A&C Black Publishers Ltd.

Griffin, J. 2001, *Food for Sport,* Peterborough; Crowood Press

Kirkham, S. 2008, *Teach Yourself Running,* London; Hodder Education

DVD

Trew, S. *Skills of Triathlon,* Peterborough; Crowood Press

Triathlon websites

www.britishtriathlon.org – This website will lead to contacts and clubs throughout the country.

www.usatriathlon.org

www.tri247.com

Triathlon magazines

220 Triathlon

Cycling weekly

Triathlon clothes and accessories

www.swimshop.co.uk

www.heartratemonitor.co.uk

www.polarpersonaltrainer.com

www.polarusa.com

www.pedometers.co.uk

www.pedometer.com

Swimming associations

www.britishswimming.org

Running methods

www.chirunning.com

www.powerrunning.com

www.posetech.com

http://running.timeoutdoors.com/classifieds/categoryList.asp?a
ct=run&ac=qs&w=189&l=&c=0&t=&p=&pcat=206

www.profeet.co.uk – For gait analysis in the UK.

Event information

British Triathlon Federation's Handbook has information on all
events throughout the year

Sports nutrition

www.nutripeople.co.uk

www.bant.org.co.uk

www.nutrition.bitwine.com

www.nctc.ul.ie/ServicesDirectory/files/National_Register_For_
Accredited_Sports_Nutritionists.doc (Ireland)

index

teach® yourself

From Advanced Sudoku to Zulu, you'll find everything you need in the **teach yourself** range, in books, on CD and on DVD.

Visit **www.teachyourself.co.uk** for more details.

Advanced Sudoku and Kakuro
Afrikaans
Alexander Technique
Algebra
Ancient Greek
Applied Psychology
Arabic
Arabic Conversation
Aromatherapy
Art History
Astrology
Astronomy
AutoCAD 2004
AutoCAD 2007
Ayurveda
Baby Massage and Yoga
Baby Signing
Baby Sleep
Bach Flower Remedies
Backgammon
Ballroom Dancing
Basic Accounting
Basic Computer Skills
Basic Mathematics
Beauty
Beekeeping
Beginner's Arabic Script
Beginner's Chinese Script
Beginner's Dutch

Beginner's French
Beginner's German
Beginner's Greek
Beginner's Greek Script
Beginner's Hindi
Beginner's Hindi Script
Beginner's Italian
Beginner's Japanese
Beginner's Japanese Script
Beginner's Latin
Beginner's Mandarin Chinese
Beginner's Portuguese
Beginner's Russian
Beginner's Russian Script
Beginner's Spanish
Beginner's Turkish
Beginner's Urdu Script
Bengali
Better Bridge
Better Chess
Better Driving
Better Handwriting
Biblical Hebrew
Biology
Birdwatching
Blogging
Body Language
Book Keeping
Brazilian Portuguese

Bridge
British Citizenship Test, The
British Empire, The
British Monarchy from Henry VIII, The
Buddhism
Bulgarian
Bulgarian Conversation
Business French
Business Plans
Business Spanish
Business Studies
C++
Calculus
Calligraphy
Cantonese
Caravanning
Car Buying and Maintenance
Card Games
Catalan
Chess
Chi Kung
Chinese Medicine
Christianity
Classical Music
Coaching
Cold War, The
Collecting
Computing for the Over 50s
Consulting
Copywriting
Correct English
Counselling
Creative Writing
Cricket
Croatian
Crystal Healing
CVs
Czech
Danish
Decluttering
Desktop Publishing
Detox
Digital Home Movie Making
Digital Photography
Dog Training
Drawing

Dream Interpretation
Dutch
Dutch Conversation
Dutch Dictionary
Dutch Grammar
Eastern Philosophy
Electronics
English as a Foreign Language
English Grammar
English Grammar as a Foreign Language
Entrepreneurship
Estonian
Ethics
Excel 2003
Feng Shui
Film Making
Film Studies
Finance for Non-Financial Managers
Finnish
First World War, The
Fitness
Flash 8
Flash MX
Flexible Working
Flirting
Flower Arranging
Franchising
French
French Conversation
French Dictionary
French for Homebuyers
French Grammar
French Phrasebook
French Starter Kit
French Verbs
French Vocabulary
Freud
Gaelic
Gaelic Conversation
Gaelic Dictionary
Gardening
Genetics
Geology
German
German Conversation

German Grammar
German Phrasebook
German Starter Kit
German Vocabulary
Globalization
Go
Golf
Good Study Skills
Great Sex
Green Parenting
Greek
Greek Conversation
Greek Phrasebook
Growing Your Business
Guitar
Gulf Arabic
Hand Reflexology
Hausa
Herbal Medicine
Hieroglyphics
Hindi
Hindi Conversation
Hinduism
History of Ireland, The
Home PC Maintenance and
    Networking
How to DJ
How to Run a Marathon
How to Win at Casino Games
How to Win at Horse Racing
How to Win at Online Gambling
How to Win at Poker
How to Write a Blockbuster
Human Anatomy & Physiology
Hungarian
Icelandic
Improve Your French
Improve Your German
Improve Your Italian
Improve Your Spanish
Improving Your Employability
Indian Head Massage
Indonesian
Instant French
Instant German
Instant Greek
Instant Italian

Instant Japanese
Instant Portuguese
Instant Russian
Instant Spanish
Internet, The
Irish
Irish Conversation
Irish Grammar
Islam
Israeli-Palestinian Conflict, The
Italian
Italian Conversation
Italian for Homebuyers
Italian Grammar
Italian Phrasebook
Italian Starter Kit
Italian Verbs
Italian Vocabulary
Japanese
Japanese Conversation
Java
JavaScript
Jazz
Jewellery Making
Judaism
Jung
Kama Sutra, The
Keeping Aquarium Fish
Keeping Pigs
Keeping Poultry
Keeping a Rabbit
Knitting
Korean
Latin
Latin American Spanish
Latin Dictionary
Latin Grammar
Letter Writing Skills
Life at 50: For Men
Life at 50: For Women
Life Coaching
Linguistics
LINUX
Lithuanian
Magic
Mahjong
Malay

Managing Stress
Managing Your Own Career
Mandarin Chinese
Mandarin Chinese Conversation
Marketing
Marx
Massage
Mathematics
Meditation
Middle East Since 1945, The
Modern China
Modern Hebrew
Modern Persian
Mosaics
Music Theory
Mussolini's Italy
Nazi Germany
Negotiating
Nepali
New Testament Greek
NLP
Norwegian
Norwegian Conversation
Old English
One-Day French
One-Day French – the DVD
One-Day German
One-Day Greek
One-Day Italian
One-Day Polish
One-Day Portuguese
One-Day Spanish
One-Day Spanish – the DVD
One-Day Turkish
Origami
Owning a Cat
Owning a Horse
Panjabi
PC Networking for Small
  Businesses
Personal Safety and Self
  Defence
Philosophy
Philosophy of Mind
Philosophy of Religion
Phone French
Phone German

Phone Italian
Phone Japanese
Phone Mandarin Chinese
Phone Spanish
Photography
Photoshop
PHP with MySQL
Physics
Piano
Pilates
Planning Your Wedding
Polish
Polish Conversation
Politics
Portuguese
Portuguese Conversation
Portuguese for Homebuyers
Portuguese Grammar
Portuguese Phrasebook
Postmodernism
Pottery
PowerPoint 2003
PR
Project Management
Psychology
Quick Fix: French Grammar
Quick Fix: German Grammar
Quick Fix: Italian Grammar
Quick Fix: Spanish Grammar
Quick Fix: Access 2002
Quick Fix: Excel 2000
Quick Fix: Excel 2002
Quick Fix: HTML
Quick Fix: Windows XP
Quick Fix: Word
Quilting
Recruitment
Reflexology
Reiki
Relaxation
Retaining Staff
Romanian
Running Your Own Business
Russian
Russian Conversation
Russian Grammar
Sage Line 50

Sanskrit
Screenwriting
Second World War, The
Serbian
Setting Up a Small Business
Shorthand Pitman 2000
Sikhism
Singing
Slovene
Small Business Accounting
Small Business Health Check
Songwriting
Spanish
Spanish Conversation
Spanish Dictionary
Spanish for Homebuyers
Spanish Grammar
Spanish Phrasebook
Spanish Starter Kit
Spanish Verbs
Spanish Vocabulary
Speaking On Special Occasions
Speed Reading
Stalin's Russia
Stand Up Comedy
Statistics
Stop Smoking
Sudoku
Swahili
Swahili Dictionary
Swedish
Swedish Conversation
Tagalog
Tai Chi
Tantric Sex
Tap Dancing
Teaching English as a Foreign
  Language
Teams & Team Working
Thai
Thai Conversation
Theatre
Time Management
Tracing Your Family History
Training
Travel Writing
Trigonometry

Turkish
Turkish Conversation
Twentieth Century USA
Typing
Ukrainian
Understanding Tax for Small
  Businesses
Understanding Terrorism
Urdu
Vietnamese
Visual Basic
Volcanoes, Earthquakes and
  Tsunamis
Watercolour Painting
Weight Control through Diet &
  Exercise
Welsh
Welsh Conversation
Welsh Dictionary
Welsh Grammar
Wills & Probate
Windows XP
Wine Tasting
Winning at Job Interviews
Word 2003
World Faiths
Writing Crime Fiction
Writing for Children
Writing for Magazines
Writing a Novel
Writing a Play
Writing Poetry
Xhosa
Yiddish
Yoga
Your Wedding
Zen
Zulu